52 LIES HEARD IN CHURCH EVERY SUNDAY

STEVE McVEY

HARVEST HOUSE PUBLISHERS
EUGENE, OREGON

Cover by Left Coast Design, Portland, Oregon

Cover photos © Thinkstock / Comstock Images / Getty Images; posztos (colorlab.hu) / Shutterstock

52 LIES HEARD IN CHURCH EVERY SUNDAY
Copyright © 2011 by Steve McVey
Published by Harvest House Publishers
Eugene, Oregon 97402
www.harvesthousepublishers.com

Library of Congress Cataloging-in-Publication Data

McVey, Steve, 1954-
52 lies heard in church every Sunday / Steve McVey.
    p. cm.
ISBN 978-0-7369-3864-8 (pbk.)
ISBN 978-0-7369-4034-4 (eBook)
    1. Preaching. 2. Bible—Hermeneutics. 3. Discernment (Christian theology) I. Title. II. Title: Fifty-two lies heard in church every Sunday.
BV4211.3.M425 2011
251'.01—dc22
                                                            2010017387

Printed in the United States of America

12 13 14 15 16 17 18 19 / BP-NI / 10 9 8 7 6 5 4

*To the many people to whom I taught
these lies for so long. May God's grace
overwhelm your hearts and minds with the
knowledge of the truth that sets us free.*

You can be assured anytime you read a book that it wasn't a solo effort on the part of the author. That's true with this book too. Many people, too many to list, have influenced my thinking through the years, thus helping to shape this book. Others were directly involved in the development of *52 Lies Heard in Church Every Sunday*.

The basis of this volume was the "101 Lies" I posted on YouTube a few years ago. Tim Stevenson took those videos and saved me a lot of time by putting them into written format. I had recorded the videos extemporaneously, and Tim did a good job of taking my sometimes-clumsy spoken sentence structure and making my words sound more articulate and well-ordered for print.

Ben Hawkins and Paul Gossard were my editors on this book and helped make it better. They were both encouraging and yet held my feet to the fire on a few things that really did need to be changed, despite my resistance early on.

Thanks to Harvest House Publishers, who has been publishing my books since 1995. I will forever be indebted to Bob Hawkins Jr., who was willing to take a chance on a young unpublished author when he published my first book, *Grace Walk*.

Appreciation for my administrative manager, Cheryl Buchanan, is a constant for me. Cheryl works tirelessly behind the scenes, handling the details of ministry so that I'm free to spend most of my time doing the things I've been gifted to do.

Anybody who knows me understands how much I adore and appreciate my wife, Melanie. She has been my greatest encourager in life since I first met her when we were both teens 40 years ago. If it all went away, I'd be okay as long as I knew she would still be by my side.

Finally, I save the best until last. I am so thankful to my heavenly Father for entrusting me with the life and ministry He has given to me. May any good that comes from this book exalt and honor Him.

Contents

Answering the Obvious Question

When you see the title *52 Lies Heard in Church Every Sunday,* your first question may be, What makes me think I'm qualified to make the judgment on what constitutes a lie? My main qualification is that I taught all these lies myself—before I began to experience a radical paradigm shift as I began to learn more and more about the meaning of grace. After two decades of travel on six continents, meeting with groups of people of every doctrinal and denominational perspective, I have come to know with certainty that I'm not alone in having taught the things addressed here.

The lies I list in this book are things I taught as a pastor at a time when I was passionate about the truth. I believe that the overwhelming majority of pastors are sincere believers who love God, the Scriptures, and the church. I have often said of myself that my heart was in the right place. It was my head that was wrong. I think that many people are in that same condition.

Frankly, I've been so wrong about so much for so long that I don't have any rocks in my pocket to throw at anybody. On the other hand, my concern and love for the church of Jesus Christ causes me to write plainly. I call these "shake 'em up to wake 'em up" statements *lies* to make the point that there has been a widespread—though admittedly unintentional—dilution of the truth. I was taught as a child that a half-truth is a whole lie. I think that applies here. When it comes to the gospel, diluted truth is polluted truth, and polluted truth is no gospel at all.

Some people will say that I'm making a big deal over nothing, arguing that my observations are nothing more than a matter of semantics. My response is that it's "only semantics" to those who don't see a difference between what I'm saying and the way it is commonly said. Words do mean something, and when ideas are put into words in such a way that they lead to or reinforce fallacious notions, it is appropriate to challenge the use of those words. Too much is at stake to risk faulty communication about the truth.

The ultimate goal? My desire is that all of us would embrace and express the pure grace of God. Pure grace points to Him, not us. It declares that whatever good may come to us is all because of His goodness, not because of anything we do or don't do. It gives Him all the credit, and us none. With that viewpoint in mind, I offer these 52 chapters in the hope that this book will cause your perception and appreciation of God's grace to grow bigger than they have ever been.

Salvation Is Giving Your Life to Christ

Beginning a book about lies taught in church presents the challenge of knowing where to start. I suppose the best place to start is at the beginning, with the most basic subject of Christianity—*salvation.* You might think it's impossible to mess this one up, but you would be wrong. I know because I messed it up for many years in my role as a senior pastor who taught the Bible every week. As I look back on how I presented the subject of salvation, I now realize I taught something seriously off base.

What was this blunder I made on so basic and fundamental an issue? I taught that the condition for salvation is "giving your life to Jesus Christ." At first glance, you may wonder how there could be anything at all wrong with that idea. After all, it's repeated from thousands of pulpits. I hope that as you consider my objection to popular teaching on the subject, you might end up agreeing that there is something wrong with it—in fact, very wrong.

Salvation is not a matter of you giving your life to Christ. In fact, it has nothing whatsoever to do with what *you* have given God. Grace revolves around what *He* has given us, not what we give to Him! You receive eternal life not because you gave Christ *your* life. You receive eternal life because He gave you *His Life!* The distinction might seem subtle, but it's important.

It is the nature of the religious perspective to focus on what we do instead of what our gracious God has done. Religionists like to think that when they behave in a certain way, God reacts to them.

Now, before I go further, let me give you a quick explanation of what I mean when I write about *religion* in this book. I have in mind the system of living by which human beings try to make themselves acceptable to God through their own actions. I realize that the apostle James used the word positively (see James 1:26-27), but as happens with many words over time, *religion* has come to mean something very different now than it did in James' time.

The English word most likely comes from the Latin *religare,* a word that actually meant "to bind fast" or "restrain." Originally, *religion* sometimes referred to people being bound together by shared beliefs. Sometimes it referred to the idea of being bound by a particular set of moral obligations. Search the definitions, and you'll see that they all have to do with the concept of being bound up.

Today, *religion* almost universally refers to a set of behavioral standards derived from a person's religious beliefs. Keep in mind this contemporary use of the word. It is this kind of religion that I'm criticizing in my observations.

I said above that religious people like to think that they can control God by their actions—that they can make God react to them. However, the truth is that the Sovereign God of the universe doesn't react to man to cause our salvation (or anything else, for that matter). He's not sitting there, on His throne in heaven, hoping with all His might that we will be so kind as to invite Him into our lives. That's the kind of religious foolishness I believed and taught for many years. I know that many others believe that way, but to hold that view isn't just a lie—it's an insult to Him. We didn't start the ball rolling regarding our salvation. He did, and to suggest otherwise diminishes Him and exalts us.

Salvation is God's work. Our response to Him is because He initiated the whole thing. We love because He first loved us. Grace means we are merely *recipients* of what He did through Jesus Christ. He is the initiator, activator, and perpetuator of our salvation. From start to finish, it's Him. We contributed nothing toward our salvation. After all, we had nothing to contribute.

The Truth Is So Much Better!

I know you may think you're a Christian because you made a decision for Christ. I thought that too—for a long time. I decided for Jesus. I asked Him into my life. It sounds noble, doesn't it? The reality, however, is that nothing could be further from the truth! I'll say it again and hope you internalize this truth: *God is the initiator of salvation.* Read the following verses, and notice how the initiation was all on God's part:

> God so loved the world, that *He gave* His only begotten Son, that whoever believes in Him shall not perish, but have eternal life (John 3:16).

> *God was in Christ reconciling the world to Himself,* not counting their trespasses against them, and He has committed to us the word of reconciliation (2 Corinthians 5:19).

> In this is love, not that we loved God, but that *He loved us and sent His Son* to be the propitiation for our sins (1 John 4:10).

Do you see the consistent theme? It's not about us. It's about Him and what He has done because of His love for us. The gospel has nothing to do with mankind reaching up to God to give Him anything. It's about the Godhead, moved by love, compassion, and mercy, reaching down to us and providing a salvation we could never have accomplished on our own. God took on flesh in the body of the Son, and empowered by the Spirit, the Son came to give us salvation. There's nothing for us to do except believe it and say, "Thank You very much!" Through faith, the objective reality of His finished work becomes our subjective reality. Consider what Paul wrote to the Ephesians:

> *By grace* you have been saved through faith; and that not of
> yourselves, it is the gift of God; not as a result of works, so
> that no one may boast (Ephesians 2:8-9).

We don't deserve, earn, or work for salvation. We simply come to
experience it through faith. According to what Paul said about the matter, we can't even take credit for the faith, for it too "is a gift of God"
and not something that we work up by our own resolve.

Clarify Your Thinking

My intention is not to plant doubt in the minds of people who've
been taught that they became Christians through giving their lives to
God. To the contrary, I want you to see that before you ever wanted
Him, He wanted you! I suspect that many—if not most—of us didn't
clearly understand all that happened when we began to follow Christ.
That's okay, though, because He has it all under control. He knows the
truth, and we can catch up in our understanding, as we are able.

I wonder if *any* of us understood how wonderful salvation really
is when we first began to follow Jesus. We can be grateful that salvation doesn't require perfect understanding on our part. God looks at
the hearts of people. He is looking for sincere hearts, not perfect heads.
Wrongheadedness on the subject may have caused us to think that becoming a Christian means we give Him our lives, but the reality is just
the opposite. He didn't come into our lives, but we entered into His
life. That's a much better arrangement in every way—don't you agree?

A misunderstanding in this area can keep you from living out your
life as intended by your Father. We are so much better prepared for life
when we begin our journey as followers of Jesus Christ by giving God all
the glory for His work, living humbly by faith in Him. Then our daily
lives become a natural extension of the way we began—a true grace walk!

Lie #2

Christians Are Just Sinners Saved by Grace

Most likely, we have all been told that we are just "sinners saved by grace." We probably hear no error repeated in church more often. The people who have believed this lie have experienced serious consequences as a result. The lie has caused devastating damage, and it has influenced countless Christians through the centuries to fall terribly short of the kind of lifestyles the Bible tells us we can live.

How could this belief cause such drastic effects? Here's why: *People will not act consistently in ways that are contrary to what they believe about themselves.* This is a foundational issue in life because it's an identity issue. The bottom line is that—over the long haul—you'll act like who you think you are. Your self-assessment will affect what you expect. Psychologists call it a self-fulfilling prophecy.

If you believe you are fundamentally a sinner, your default setting will be to act like a sinner. To behave in any other way would be to act inconsistently with the person you perceive yourself to be. After all, what do you expect a "sinner" to do? *Sin.* Sinning is simply the normal behavior for a sinner. That's one of the reasons why many of us have so often fallen woefully short of the possibility of the victorious living the

Bible teaches we can enjoy, and it's why critics of our faith have so often scoffed at our claims of transformed lives. Our walk doesn't match our talk, but how can it when we see ourselves at the core as sinners?

Constantly trying to behave in a way that doesn't seem natural will wear anybody out. That's why we must know the truth about who we are. Truth is not determined by our feelings, the opinions of others, or our behavior. It's determined by who *God* says we are!

The Truth Is So Much Better!

To understand salvation properly, we have to first clearly understand mankind's need for salvation. Before we trusted Christ, our problem wasn't that we needed forgiveness. Instead, we needed to understand and believe in the resurrection power of Jesus Christ and God's ability to transform us by that power. *We were dead to the reality of His finished work and in need to believe in what He accomplished.*

Jesus came into a world of people who were surely in need of forgiveness, but that wasn't our only problem. In fact, it wasn't even our biggest problem. What do dead men need? There is only one answer—life! Paul described what took place:

> But God, being rich in mercy, because of His great love with which He loved us, even when we were dead in our transgressions, *made us alive together with Christ* (by grace you have been saved) (Ephesians 2:4-5).

In the process of making us alive in Christ, God didn't just revamp the old creation. He created something brand-new by causing our old life to die and giving us a new one in its place! "Therefore if anyone is in Christ, he is a *new creature;* the old things passed away; behold, new things have come" (2 Corinthians 5:17).

The word *creature* has *create* as its root, which means "to bring something into existence out of nothing." In Christ, you are no longer a sinner. Paul told the Galatians that God put the sinner to death with Jesus Christ on the cross and created somebody brand-new:

I have been crucified with Christ; *and it is no longer I who live, but Christ lives in me;* and the life which I now live in the flesh I live by faith in the Son of God, who loved me and gave Himself up for me (Galatians 2:20).

What did Paul mean when he wrote, "It is no longer I who live"? He meant that God took old Sinner Saul, whose spiritual roots had come from the sinful family of Adam, and crucified him with Jesus Christ, putting that old man to death once and for all. Then through Christ's resurrection, He raised him up, recreated him as Saint Paul, and put him into the righteous family of Jesus Christ.

The same thing happened to you. You were included in the work of Christ on the cross just as Paul was. You aren't a sinner anymore. Nobody is suggesting that you never sin, but what you *do* doesn't define who you *are*. I could act like a woman, but that kind of ridiculous behavior wouldn't change the reality of who I am. I'm a man because I was born a man. It's birth—not behavior—that gives us our identity. In Christ, you've been made a saint. You now have the righteousness of Jesus Christ as your own, and you have a new identity. You're not a sinner anymore. The sinner is dead, having been crucified with Christ. Now you are a child of God!

Ephesians 2:10 says that you are God's "workmanship." The Greek word for "workmanship"—related to the later English term *poem*—often referred to a work of art of various kinds. The New Living Translation says that you are "a divine masterpiece," created in Christ Jesus. The New Testament calls you a *saint* 63 times. *Saint* means "holy one," the result of God's work. Consider these two verses:

Paul…to the church of God which is at Corinth, to those who have been *sanctified* in Christ Jesus, *saints* by calling (1 Corinthians 1:1-2).

By this will we have been *sanctified* through the offering of the body of Jesus Christ once for all (Hebrews 10:10).

Calling us "sanctified" or "saints" is not a reference to behavior, but to identity. Make no mistake about it: You are a saint in Jesus Christ. If you want to walk in freedom, you must believe the Bible on this one. You are who you are—whether you believe it or not. But believing this truth will set you free to live the life you were created to enjoy.

You may wonder, then, why the apostle Paul said once that he was the chief of sinners. To answer that point, it's important to realize this: If Paul were claiming to be a sinner in a "saved" state, he would be contradicting what he said about his identity in Christ in many other verses. So he couldn't mean that.

What is the answer? Think of it this way: Throughout his boxing career, Muhammad Ali has claimed to be "the champion of the world!" Ironically, he maintains that claim to this day, even though he hasn't boxed for years. But nobody calls him a liar. After all, they know he means that nobody has ever surpassed his record, which he still holds. He *is* the boxing champion of the world.

That's what Paul meant when he said he was the chief of sinners. He wasn't saying that he still out-sinned everybody. Because he was in Christ, Paul did not have the identity of a sinner, and he didn't see himself that way. He simply meant that before he knew Christ, nobody had topped his sinning record. It was something he never forgot: As a Pharisee, he had persecuted Christians by putting them in prison even to death. After his experience on the road to Damascus, he never got over his sense of the amazing grace that saved him. Neither should we.

Clarify Your Thinking

The idea that you are just a sinner saved by grace is a lie. It falls far short of the truth of the New Testament, which repeatedly says that we are saints. It also says that we have been *sanctified* (made saints) by the finished work of Jesus Christ. We really need to get this one right. If we don't, we'll never live the triumphant life that is our birthright.

Over the long haul, our behavior tells a lot about what we believe about ourselves. When we recognize who we really are, our lifestyle will glorify Him more and more. We aren't sinners! By Christ's work, we have been transformed into new creatures called saints.

Once we understand that, we become motivated to live saintly lives—not to be confused with religious lifestyles. You're not just a sinner saved by grace. Shake off that lie and affirm the truth about your identity in Christ.

Do you see the importance of making this distinction between your life being changed versus it being exchanged? The former would suggest that now you are simply an "improved you," which isn't at all the case. You are a new you! Every residue of the old sinful spiritual DNA you inherited from Adam was crucified. It is dead and buried! You have been raised to "walk in newness of life" (Romans 6:4) because Christ is your very life source now.

This understanding of salvation puts the finished work of the cross in its proper perspective. Jesus didn't come to straighten up the mess Adam made. He came to *undo* the damage done in the garden by totally reversing its effect in our lives. In Adam, we became sinners, but the finished work of Christ does much more than change us by cleaning us up from our sin. His work took our old life in Adam and put it away forever. Hebrews 9:26 says that He came to "*put away sin* by the sacrifice of Himself."

Your sins aren't just forgiven now. They're gone! In the wonderful imagery of the Psalms, "As far as the east is from the west, so far has He removed our transgressions from us" (Psalm 103:12). The apostle Paul explained how God did this: "He made Him who knew no sin to be sin on our behalf, so that we might become the righteousness of God in Him" (2 Corinthians 5:21).

Look carefully at what this verse says. Our Father took our sins and gave them to the sinless Christ, who is the basis of our forgiveness. He took our sins away and separated them from us as far as the east is from the west. But that's not all! He also took the righteousness of Jesus Christ and gave it to us! That's the basis of our justification, which is our verdict of "not guilty" before the Supreme Judge of all. There again you see that God's work in Christ is not just a change but also a *total exchange*. Debunking the lie that God changed you and embracing the full truth about the matter will liberate you to rise up to your full potential as His transformed child.

Lie #4

Becoming a Christian Means Having Your Sins Forgiven

Ask most believers to explain what it means to be a Christian, and they will tell you that it means having their sins forgiven. Many of us have held that viewpoint since the moment we first trusted Christ. True, our sins have been forgiven as a result of the finished work of Christ on the cross, but that is in no way the essence of salvation. Becoming a Christian is much more than that. In fact, God's act in forgiving our sins is actually a secondary matter to Him and not the most important thing.

As great as it is, Jesus came to do more than provide forgiveness. When a person trusts Christ and realizes that his sins are forgiven, that is a good thing—as far as his past is concerned. But that would still leave us in a vulnerable situation when it comes to our present and our future. By what power could we go free from the power of sin today? And what about the sins we will commit in the future? Forgiveness of our sins is a wonderful thing, but that alone would not have power to transform our lives.

Jesus Christ came to give us Divine Life, *His* Life. He said in John 10:10, "I came that they may have life, and have it abundantly." The fact that our sins have been forgiven should never be minimized. We thank God for that, but if that is the extent of our understanding, we will find ourselves falling far short of living up to the full potential we have in Christ.

Becoming a Christian happens when by faith you recognize that your life and the life of Jesus have merged together into one. The idea that Christianity is merely about having our sins forgiven has led many people to experience an anemic walk in their daily lives. They know they have been born again and are on their way to heaven, but because they fail to understand that the primary aspect of salvation is realizing the subjective experience of Christ's indwelling life, they see their lives here on earth as time in a waiting room, where they stay until it's time to go to heaven.

The Truth Is So Much Better!

The message of the gospel must include both the cross *and* the resurrection. By the crucifixion of Jesus Christ, forgiveness came to us, but that's only half the gospel. The rest of the news is found at the site of an empty tomb. When He arose, we arose with Him to a new life. That aspect of the gospel makes possible the abundant life Jesus promised that He came to give us. Once we understand the complete truth of the gospel—that salvation means that we receive the life of Christ—we become equipped to live the life He came to give us.

We have seen previously that the problem humanity had in Adam was not only that we were guilty and in need of forgiveness. We were *dead* and in need of life: "And you were *dead* in your trespasses and sins" (Ephesians 2:1). That's why God's solution also had to provide for man's state of spiritual death, as well as his state of guilt. And Jesus Christ has provided a full salvation:

> Therefore we have been buried with Him through baptism into death, so that as Christ was raised from the dead through the glory of the Father, so we too might walk in *newness of life*. For if we have been united with Him in the likeness of His

death, certainly we shall also be in the likeness of His resurrection (Romans 6:4-5).

You see the cross and resurrection working together in Paul's description in Colossians 2:13:

> When you were *dead* in your transgressions and the uncircumcision of your flesh, *He made you alive together with Him,* having *forgiven us all our transgressions.*

Clarify Your Thinking

The idea that salvation *equals* "having our sins forgiven" is a half-truth, and a half-truth equates to a whole lie because it leads to an incorrect conclusion. You have received divine life that indwells you and seeks to find expression through you at this very moment. God did not intend Christ's work of salvation merely to be about getting you into heaven. As someone has said, "Christ didn't come just to get men out of hell and into heaven. He came to get Himself out of heaven and into men."

The indwelling Holy Spirit means that we possess *Christ's empowering presence* every hour of every day. This is the foundation for living the way God intends. Understanding that "the kingdom of God is within you" empowers us for more than just waiting to go to heaven. It equips us to live as citizens of heaven moment by moment in the meantime—between now and when we actually cross the borderline between time and eternity. We don't just have forgiveness. We have the dynamic life of the living Savior within us, enabling us to live out His life in this world.

Lie #5

Our Sins Are Under the Blood of Jesus

Just as there are trite statements in all cultures that sound true on the surface but don't necessarily convey the truth, so it is in the church world. We've heard some things said in church that have been stated so often and sound so logical that we believe they must be true. This is one of those statements. Take a close look at that statement: Your sins are under the blood of Jesus. What could possibly be wrong with that?

To clear up a lot of confusion, ask this simple question: "What do you mean by that?" Ask people what they mean by a phrase or term, and you'll finally be able to pinpoint what the controversy or teaching is really saying. You'll often discover that you actually agree with what a person is trying to say, even though you disagree with how they say it. At other times, you'll discover that what sounds good on the surface actually disguises a serious error beneath. Either way, you won't discover what you're really dealing with until you ask people to clarify what they mean. Many of our shorthand expressions and clichés serve to promote errors and reinforce misunderstandings.

In this case, what someone usually *means* by saying that our sins are under the blood of Jesus is that we are forgiven. I would certainly do nothing but agree with that assertion, but I do have a problem with this way of trying to say it. It communicates a serious misunderstanding about the work of Christ.

The Truth Is So Much Better!

It is important to understand a major difference between the old and new covenants and how they describe the process of sacrifice and forgiveness. In the Old Testament period under the Law of Moses, forgiveness was indeed offered to the people, but the dominant concept was that the blood of the sacrifices covered their sins.

You may remember how the priests would offer sacrificial animals for the sins of Israel. There were many, many types of sacrifices, offered continually. There were daily, weekly, monthly, and yearly sacrifices. The most important day of worship for ancient Israel was the annual observance *Yom Kippur*—literally, "the Day of Atonement." This was the one and only day of the year when a human representative, the high priest, would enter the Holy of Holies, the innermost room of the tabernacle or temple, and approach the Ark of the Covenant. When the blood of an innocent animal was poured on the Ark, the judgment seat became the mercy seat. Men's sins were considered "covered" by the blood, and the people were counted forgiven by God—but just for the moment, that is, because no sacrifice under the Law ever provided for *tomorrow's* sins. At best, those sacrifices were temporary.

However, things have changed with the coming of the new covenant. The Law's observances were only shadows and previews of the work of Christ, who would accomplish a far greater work.

> Therefore it was necessary for the copies of the things in the heavens to be cleansed with these, but the heavenly things themselves with *better sacrifices* than these (Hebrews 9:23).

Jesus' offering of Himself was truly a "better sacrifice," but there are powerful implications in that assertion that many Christians don't yet know. Remember the scene when Jesus showed up at the Jordan

River where John the Baptist was baptizing? John said, "Behold, the Lamb of God who *takes away* the sin of the world!" (John 1:29). That old covenant prophet John understood better than many new covenant Christians today that Jesus came to do something different than previous priests had done. He didn't come to hide away our sins from God's sight by putting them under the blood of a sacrifice. He came to do away with them completely. As John wrote, "You know that He appeared in order to *take away* sins" (1 John 3:5).

The book of Hebrews teaches that Jesus was an infinitely better sacrifice than any of those offered in the Old Testament. In fact, He was the perfect sacrifice. When He offered Himself for our sins, His shed blood didn't just "cover" our sins. By His sacrifice, our sins were *taken away.*

Note what Hebrews 9:26 says:

> Now *once* at the consummation of the ages He has been manifested to *put away sin* by the sacrifice of Himself.

The words *put away* are one word in the Greek language, which means "to disannul, to do away with, to completely destroy." Jesus didn't come to cover your sins. *He came to take your sin away,* and that's exactly what He did.

The writer of Hebrews makes this point unmistakably clear:

> Every [old covenant] priest stands daily ministering and offering time after time the same sacrifices, which can never take away sins; but He, having offered one sacrifice for all time, sat down at the right hand of God...For by one offering He has perfected for all time those who are sanctified (Hebrews 10:11-12,14).

Clarify Your Thinking

So it's actually great news to know that your sins are *not* under the blood of Christ. His blood doesn't cover them. The blood of Jesus Christ has taken your sins away!

Some have said that the doctrine of justification is the teaching that because of Christ's finished work, our status can be described as though we never sinned. It's really more than that, but that's a good start. In the eyes of your heavenly Father, you have an unblemished record. He isn't overlooking anything. He has rewritten your history by taking away the sins of your past, present, and future and giving you the history of Christ Himself.

Believing that your sins are "under the blood of Christ" doesn't truly honor the finished work of Jesus. Ironically, it actually *diminishes* His sacrifice. What He did is much greater than most people have understood. He doesn't condemn us for our sins now. And here's why: There are no sins to condemn. The cross has obliterated them!

Your sins have been blotted out, and you have been given the righteousness of God in Christ. You don't ever need to be bogged down with a preoccupation about sins again. Instead, you can now walk in the confidence of knowing that your life isn't defined by sin anymore, but by the righteousness of the Christ who has become your very life.

It may sound good to say that our sins are under the blood of Jesus Christ, but it is a lie. The Bible says our sins have been taken away from us, forever, by the finished work of Christ at the cross.

Lie #6

Your Greatest
Need Is to
Love God More

One time a lawyer came to Jesus and asked Him, "Teacher, which is the great commandment in the Law?" Note the focus of the man's question here. He was asking about *the Law.* Jesus answered his question, saying,

> "You shall love the Lord your God with all your heart, and with all your soul, and with all your mind." This is the great and foremost commandment (Matthew 27:37-38).

In response to the man's question about the greatest law, Jesus answered that it is to love God. Therefore, what could be wrong with telling people they need to love God more? Once again, with some probing we find that what sounds good on the surface doesn't work in real life. So what's the answer?

Simple. By our own power, we can't love God the way that command demands. God knew this, of course, which is one of the reasons He gave the commandment. Just try commanding your children to love each other more. It might be right and a good thing to want, but commanding people to love just doesn't work. Commanding people who don't already possess love *to love* does nothing but expose their inability.

Remember, Jesus was quoting the Law of Moses to people who were under the Law. Pushing the idea that we need to love God more is right in line with the Law. Although it sounds good on the surface, it is actually legalistic teaching. It's an ironic fact that when a person focuses on the demand to love God more, the whole thing actually backfires and causes him to become painfully aware of how much he lacks in the area of loving God.

That's the weakness of laws. They are true and right about what we *ought* to do—but there is no power in them to *enable* us to do!

The Truth Is So Much Better!

The Bible says that when the Law of God confronts us, the result is that it *stirs up more* sinful passions. Look at these passages:

> The Law came in so that the transgression would *increase* (Romans 5:20).

> While we were in the flesh, the sinful passions, *which were aroused by the Law,* were at work in the members of our body to bear fruit for death (Romans 7:5).

> What shall we say then? Is the Law sin? May it never be! On the contrary, I would not have come to know sin except through the Law; for I would not have known about coveting if the Law had not said, "You shall not covet." But sin, *taking opportunity through the commandment,* produced in me coveting of every kind; for apart from the Law sin is dead (Romans 7:7-8).

The Law stimulates rebellion against the very thing it demands. So if you focus on how much you *should* love God, that command will condemn you and cause you to be filled with a sense of guilt. In fact, people often feel that they *ought* to love God more already. So why don't they? They can't. So what is the answer? It's right there in 1 John 4:19: "We love, because He first loved us." It isn't possible to love Him as we want to until we understand how much He loves us. Then, and only then, we will find love for God swelling up within our hearts.

Haven't you found this to be true in your own life? When you've focused on loving Him more, did you feel like you were succeeding? Or did you find yourself literally praying for help to love Him more? Praying, "Lord, help me to love you more" is evidence that you felt you were falling short in that area.

The key to loving God more, then, is to focus on how much He loves us, not on how much we love Him at any given moment in life. Shake free from the lie that the most important thing in your life is to love God more and begin to focus on how much your heavenly Father loves you.

This is why Paul mentions so often in his letters his desire that those to whom he wrote would gain the spiritual understanding of God's love for them. I suggest you pray the same thing for yourself that you can see in this great passage:

> I bow my knees before the Father, from whom every family in heaven and on earth derives its name, that He would grant you, according to the riches of His glory, to be strengthened with power through His Spirit in the inner man, so that Christ may dwell in your hearts through faith; and that you, being rooted and grounded in love, *may be able to comprehend* with all the saints what is the breadth and length and height and depth, and *to know the love of Christ which surpasses knowledge,* that you may be filled up to all the fullness of God (Ephesians 3:14-19).

I promise you: People who are growing to know deeply the transforming love of God in Jesus Christ in their hearts and minds find that loving God in return comes without need of His command. These are the people who begin discovering what a grace perspective accomplishes in our lives—without a struggle.

Clarify Your Thinking

As you grow in your understanding of the great love that He has for you, you'll discover an awakening and motivation within you. In response to His love, you will grow and flourish. You'll find yourself loving Him more and more (and even loving everybody else around you more and more too).

The idea that the greatest need in your life is to love God more may sound true on the surface, but it is a legalistic lie. The Bible says that God loves us, and everything revolves around that. When you focus on His love for you—instead of your love for Him—you will discover that knowing the love of God for you is a truth that will set you free in your own grace walk.

Lie #7

The Answer for Weak Christian Commitment Is to Rededicate Your Life to Christ

During my years of legalistic teaching in the church, perhaps more often than anything else, I challenged people to rededicate themselves to Christ. I believed we all needed to try harder and be more sincere and zealous in our efforts to live for Him. I rededicated myself until I felt worn out from it at times.

Rededication isn't the grace way. The real answer to a sense of need in our walk with God isn't to promise Him that we'll try harder. That's true even though we may rededicate ourselves. Although many people are sincere in their rededication to Christ, it is a wrong approach to the desire to be more consistent in our commitment to Him.

The problem with rededicating ourselves to Christ is *self,* which is really just another word for the self-sufficiency of the flesh. The essence of religious flesh, as strange as it might seem, is our *trying* to live the Christian life. That is what actually prevents us from living the Christian life. In fact, the harder we try, the greater the likelihood that we won't succeed because victory in the Christian life doesn't come by trying. It comes by trusting.

The Truth Is So Much Better!

Self-determination, self-discipline, self-sufficiency—those are what stand in the way. Jesus is the way to victory in your grace walk. Notice what Jesus says about following Him:

> If anyone wishes to come after Me, he must deny himself, and take up his cross and follow Me (Matthew 16:24).

What did He say we are to do? Dedicate ourselves to Him? No, He said that we are to *deny* self.

Rededicating ourselves to try harder isn't the answer. It doesn't matter how sincere we might be. It simply won't work. The answer is to trust Him. That's the only cure for an unstable, up-and-down spiritual existence.

Jesus illustrated our relationship with Him by comparing us to a branch:

> I am the vine, you are the branches; he who abides in Me and I in him, he bears much fruit, for apart from Me you can do nothing (John 15:5).

Think about the relationship between a vine and branch. Can a branch *produce* fruit? No. If you need proof, just cut a branch off a vine or fruit tree, and watch awhile to see how much fruit is produced. However, if a branch is attached to the source with a flow of life, it can *bear* fruit. The branch is a great "fruit hanger," but it is incapable of producing fruit on its own.

That is a perfect representation of our ability to live the Christian life. We cannot produce it; no matter how hard we try, no matter how "dedicated" we are. But we can *bear the characteristics of Christ's life* by remaining dependent on Him and allowing Him access to our humanity through faith.

As we have seen before, becoming a Christian has to do with much more than forgiveness. It is a whole new life, the life of Christ. That's why, after describing our death and resurrection in Christ, Paul calls on us to think and act accordingly on the basis of that life:

Consider yourselves to be dead to sin, but alive to God in Christ Jesus. Therefore do not let sin reign in your mortal body so that you obey its lusts, and do not go on presenting the members of your body to sin as instruments of unrighteousness; but *present yourselves to God as those alive from the dead,* and your members as instruments of righteousness to God. For sin shall not be master over you, for you are not under law but under grace (Romans 6:11-14).

Our Father wants us to learn that the Christian life is not *hard* for us to live; it is *impossible.* You won't ever live a victorious Christian life by rededicating yourself to God, and telling Him you're going to try harder to do a better job. Instead, we must come to the end of ourselves, our self-life. We need to say, "Lord, it's not just hard for me to live a life that honors You, it is impossible for me to do it. I will stop trying and just trust You. You are my life. Now, Lord Jesus, live Your life through me."

Is there a place for our active participation in Christian living? Absolutely! But it is vitally important to have that will and effort exercised in an attitude totally dependent on God's power within us. The relationship between them is clearly shown in this passage: "So then, my beloved...work out your salvation with fear and trembling" (Philippians 2:12).

That sure sounds like dedicated effort, doesn't it? Yes, but the next verse, completing the sentence, tells the inner secret, the hidden source of power for the outward effort: "For it is God who is at work in you, both to will and to work for His good pleasure" (Philippians 2:13).

In other words, the life my creator has designed for me can be understood as Him expressing His life through me from the inside until it governs my life on the outside. I depend on Him as my life, my wisdom, and my power as I walk through life.

Clarify Your Thinking

We didn't become Christians by revving up our religious RPMs and trying to make progress toward entering God's kingdom by what we did. Instead, we came to the place where we realized there was nothing we could or even *had* to do to get into a right standing with God. We realized that He had already done it all. Nothing has changed in that regard now that you are following Jesus.

We are to simply acknowledge that—no matter how hard we might try—we can do nothing to make ourselves stronger. Just like when we trusted Him when we experienced salvation, we have to come to Him in faith and total dependence that He will be the One who does what needs to be done. And He will.

The apostle Paul said, "As you have received Christ Jesus the Lord, *so walk in Him*" (Colossians 2:6). We continue the walk in the same way we started it—by grace, through faith. If we sense that we are weak in our commitment to Him, the answer is to trust in His grace and know that He is committed to us. The One who began a good work in you will finish what He has started. Just trust Him, knowing it's not up to you and how hard you try. Faith is the key. That's all it takes.

The Holy Spirit Convicts Unbelievers of Their Sins

How are we to pray for a friend or family member who doesn't believe in Christ? If you follow the example of most believers' prayers, you'll pray that the Holy Spirit will convict them of their sins so that they'll become open to the gospel. No one would object to the motivation behind that kind of prayer, which is the salvation of loved ones. But are we really praying according to what the Bible says the Holy Spirit will do when we approach it that way?

The answer is no. It is pointless to hope or pray that the Holy Spirit will convict an unbeliever of the things they are doing wrong. He's not going to do that for one simple reason: Their sins are not the problem. Christ dealt with their sins on the cross. When He said, "It is finished," He was including the world, not just those who have already believed the gospel. You see, the specific sins—the detailed misbehavior—of a person who isn't trusting in Jesus Christ are just indicative of a deeper problem.

The Holy Spirit isn't going to convict unbelievers of their specific sins because that wouldn't meet the deepest need they have. Their biggest problem isn't their misbehavior. He's going to convict them of the one thing that ultimately matters—their unbelief in Christ. That's the core issue.

The Truth Is So Much Better!

John 16:8 tells us exactly what the Holy Spirit will do in regard to the conviction of the world. Jesus said, "He, when He comes, will convict the world concerning sin and righteousness and judgment; concerning sin, *because they do not believe in Me*" (John 16:8-9).

The word *convict* in this biblical context doesn't mean that He finds them guilty as we might normally think when we use that word. The word in this context means "to convince," and that's what God wants to do. God's Spirit will convince an unbeliever of his unbelief, and he will come to see the necessity of believing in Jesus Christ and what He has done on that person's behalf. In comparison to that, nothing else matters. Compared to unbelief, behavior is just incidental.

I'll give you an example. When I was in high school, I worked in a nursing home. Part of my responsibility there was to take the bodies of men who had died and then bathe and clean those corpses to get them ready for the funeral director.

When I bathed, shaved, and dressed them, I would tie up their dead bodies in a geriatrics chair. There they would sit until the funeral home would come to pick them up and take them to the morgue. Without wanting to sound disrespectful, I can honestly say that after I finished with them, most of those guys looked better than I'd seen them look in years. Everything looked right about them, but they had a big problem. They were dead.

That's exactly the way it is with the life of an unbeliever. His sins, as serious as those things might be in terms of how they will affect his life, are really symptoms. You might as well forget praying that the Holy Spirit will convict an unbeliever of his addiction to drugs, or her addiction to alcohol or promiscuity or anything like that. If a person doesn't know Christ, he has one consuming problem, and that is his unbelief.

Clarify Your Thinking

Sometimes the most glaring characteristic of an unbeliever in our minds may be his misbehavior. We may cringe when we see a person acting in a way that is considered morally offensive to many people, but that isn't the big thing to God. He knew how we would all behave back when He gave Himself for our sins. His concern now is that we believe on Him and enter into the experience of knowing our sins are forgiven and living out of the fullness of His indwelling life. The Holy Spirit will convict an unbeliever of only one thing—his unbelief in Jesus Christ. He will show that person where he stands so that he can enter into the experience of knowing God through Jesus.

We all know people who haven't trusted in Jesus Christ. When we pray for them, let's not pray that they'll be convicted about taking drugs, drunkenness, immorality, or anything like that. Let's pray that the Holy Spirit will convict them of their unbelief, because that is His ministry. When we pray for them in that way, we are appropriating a truth of the Bible that can make an eternal difference in somebody's life.

The Christian Life Is All of Him and None of Me

Here's another lie that seems right at first glance. If a person doesn't know any better, it could almost sound like an expression of genuine humility. That's why so many people are inclined to believe it: "The Christian life is all of Christ and none of me." This statement almost sounds super spiritual, but it's still a lie.

Your life is not all of Him and none of you. Think about it this way: When Jesus came into this world in human form, was it all of God and none of Him? No, to the contrary—it was all of God and all of Him. Jesus and His Father were in complete union so that He was 100 percent man and 100 percent God at the same time.

Theologians call that phenomenon the *hypostatic union,* which means that Jesus was not 50 percent man and 50 percent God. He was 100 percent God and 100 percent man. He was the God-man. So as a man, Jesus might have said, "It's all of God and all of Me."

Now, even though Jesus *is* God, while you and I are not, we have come into union with God through Christ. Our very existence resides in Jesus Christ, and we have fellowship with God through Him by the ministry of the Holy Spirit.

The Truth Is So Much Better!

First Corinthians 6:17 says that the one who has joined himself together with the Lord is one spirit with Him. It's not partly Him and partly us that defines our lives. I've heard people pray, "Lord, I just want more of You." Maybe they mean something different from what they're saying, but the fact is that we already have *all* of Him residing in us.

The apostle Paul wrote that "in Him all the fullness of Deity dwells in bodily form, and in Him you have been made complete" (Colossians 2:9-10). We lack nothing. Jesus Christ possesses all of God the Father. We possess all of Jesus Christ. He possesses all of us. It's a complete union—there's no division between us.

In John 17, Jesus prayed and asked His Father that we might be one with each other just as He and the Father are one. Then He prayed that we would be in them (17:20-21). We know that the Father always answers His Son's requests, so the reality now is that, just as the Father, Son, and Spirit are one, we are one with Him too.

The Bible's message is not "Christ *instead of* your life," as if it's a matter of a replacement in which He swallows up our humanity and we don't exist anymore. Nor is it just "Christ *in* your life," as if it were a matter of having a divine additive that enhances our humanity. It is Christ *as* your life. He is in us. We are in Him. So it is all of Him in us, but it's also all of us in Him. There's the oneness.

Clarify Your Thinking

If you believe that "it's all Christ and none of you," it can be very easy to become passive in your daily lifestyle. You could easily say, "Well, I'm only a conduit, and I just wait for Him to do it through me. He does it all, and I do nothing." That perspective fails to recognize the nature of the union we share with Christ.

We are colaborers together with God. We put our neck in the same yoke with Jesus. He said, "Take My yoke upon you." Together, as colaborers with God and empowered by Him, we move forward. As He acts through our personalities and physical bodies, we act. He activates the will in your mind, but He does it *through you.* Not "instead of you." It's 100 percent Him and 100 percent us, and we move in sync as His Spirit leads us.

You Can Go Too Far with Grace

The people who are afraid of the message of the grace walk have sometimes suggested that you can go too far with grace. They're worried about what might happen if we do that. This lie finds expression out of that unfounded fear.

We need to remember that grace involves God expressing His unconditional love and favor toward us, independent of anything we ever do or don't do. Grace is personified in Jesus. So to say that you can go too far with grace is like saying that you can go too far with Jesus. It simply isn't possible. Consider this: God is infinite in His goodness, holiness, and love. Can He "go too far" with those?

Some people are afraid that if you teach the pure grace of God, people might be encouraged to go out and sin. That kind of fear shows a lack of clear understanding about what grace does in a person's life. When God's grace really takes hold of us, it does the exact opposite of encouraging sin. It causes us to draw near in love and faith to God, which is where we find a greater desire to walk in a manner pleasing to Him.

The idea that you can go too far with grace is an irrational fear. When we sin, we are acting in a *disgraceful* way. We are contradicting the very essence of the grace of God. Grace empowers us to honor our Father through our actions, not dishonor Him. It is possible to pervert grace so that it stops being grace, but it isn't possible to go too far with it.

So when people ask me, "Aren't you afraid that by teaching the grace of God so strongly, you will encourage people to sin?" I answer, "Not if you teach it in the way the Bible teaches it."

The Truth Is So Much Better!

Paul explained the effect of grace this way:

> For if by the transgression of the one [Adam], death reigned through the one, much more those who receive the abundance of grace and of the gift of righteousness will reign in life through the One, Jesus Christ (Romans 5:17).

He said that if we're going to reign in life, there needs to be an abundance of grace. That abundance has provided the gift of righteousness. When we understand that, the result will be that we reign in life, which surely does not sound like an encouragement to keep sinning.

The word *abundance* in that verse suggests an overflow. It doesn't mean filling something to the top. It means filling it beyond the top so that it spills over. Paul says that is what has happened to us. We have received an overflow of grace.

In Philippians 3, Paul tells his own story of what receiving the grace of Jesus Christ did for him. He could point to his own religious credentials, which all his contemporaries would have considered stellar, but he threw it all away in exchange for the joy of knowing Jesus Christ. Then did he stop there? No. Notice what he says:

> Not that I have already obtained it or have already become perfect, but I press on so that I may lay hold of that for which also I was laid hold of by Christ Jesus. Brethren, I do not regard myself as having laid hold of it yet; but one thing I do: forgetting what lies behind and reaching forward to

what lies ahead, I press on toward the goal for the prize of the upward call of God in Christ Jesus (Philippians 3:12-14).

Paul is clear about the fact that God's grace motivated him to press on toward a deeper knowledge and intimacy with Jesus Christ. He wasn't concerned about getting out of balance with grace. He knew that when we have gone as far as we can imagine in our understanding and experiencing of God's grace, we haven't exhausted it! God's grace reaches further than we can imagine.

Clarify Your Thinking

Go too far with grace? There's no way. Most people haven't gone *far enough* in their understanding of it. We need an overflow of grace, especially in the modern church world. Especially in the lives of those who've been ambushed by legalistic religion that has caused them to wrongly imagine that God's biggest concern is over what they're doing and not doing. Legalism puts a person on that behavior-oriented track. It's trying to live by the Law, and it's a dead-end road from which our Father wants to deliver us by revealing the truth to us. Many people may say they don't want to live under the Law, but they're scared to death of what they think is the grace of God. That's why we need to teach them what it really means.

We need to boldly proclaim God's grace to the religious world—not just to those who don't profess faith in Christ, but also to the church world. Even if you could go too far with grace—*which you can't*—I've not been around anybody yet who had even a remote possibility of going too far with the grace of God.

Go too far with grace? Not a chance. We *need* an abundance of grace in the legalistic barrenness of the modern church. It's only when we jump in over our heads into the river of God's grace and experience that abundance that we know the victory that is ours in Jesus Christ.

Your Greatest Responsibility Is to Serve God

Listen to the average sermon in the average church building on a Sunday, and it's almost inevitable that you'll come away believing that the most important thing about your relationship to God is your spiritual service. Service is the battle cry of legalistic religion. Many people believe it's the very reason why they were brought to faith in Jesus Christ. The motto "saved to serve" has found a nesting place in too many places in the modern church world.

This erroneous idea is shared among all religions, even among the most primitive pagans. People who practiced ancient pagan religions often went to great lengths to appease their gods. After all, angry gods might do really bad things. Their focus was all about placating their gods by giving them sacrifices. To keep people in line, people told stories about the gods getting angry and hurling bolts of divine judgment on those who dared to neglect doing what was expected. Angry gods might hit you with a plague, earthquake, or famine if you're not careful.

This is the pathetic reality: In the modern days, with a complete Bible telling us the truth of the matter, there are many who still hold that pagan viewpoint. They really think that if they don't live up to the demands they imagine that God places on them, something terrible may happen to them. As a result, their lot in life becomes trying to stay on God's good side by doing what He expects.

Some would argue, "I don't serve God because I'm afraid of Him. I do it because it's my responsibility toward Him." That view is related to the same fear motivation I've described. To think that God is interested in what we do for Him is bizarre in light of what the Bible actually teaches.

There is a fundamental error embedded in this kind of thinking. It's the idea that God *needs* anything you or I have to give. We're talking about an Almighty God here! What could He possibly need us to do?

Just like today, Christian history is full of stories of believers who desperately worked to serve God. There's no doubting their sincerity or effort. But there is a serious problem with someone's conception of God when He is seen as an employer or master whose interest in us is based on what we have to offer to the relationship.

The Truth Is So Much Better!

Your greatest responsibility has nothing to do with serving God. In fact, when Paul addressed the pagans on Mars Hill, here's what he had to say about the notion that our God needs something from us.

> The God who made the world and all things in it, since He is Lord of heaven and earth, does not dwell in temples made with hands; *nor is He served by human hands, as though He needed anything,* since He Himself gives to all people, life and breath and all things (Acts 17:24-25).

God is a Giver. He is utterly self-sufficient, the only Being who truly needs nothing. He doesn't need man to do things for Him. One time He explained it like this: "If I were hungry I would not tell you, for the world is Mine, and all it contains" (Psalm 50:12). That statement almost sounds like a sort of divine humor. Imagine God saying, "If I wanted something to eat, I wouldn't bother mentioning it to you because you couldn't do a single thing about it!"

Clarify Your Thinking

This reality is a bad news/good news proposition. The bad news is that God doesn't need you. Sorry, but there's nothing you have that He needs. What could we possibly think God needs us to do to serve Him? He's the One who spoke the world into existence. If we think God needs us, we either greatly overestimate our own value and contribution or else greatly underestimate His ability to do what needs to be done.

I said it's a bad news/good news proposition. Here's the good news: God *wants* you! He isn't looking for a maid, but He does want a bride—and that means you.

Does service not fit into the picture at all? Of course it does, but we serve from an overflow of the love we have for Him. Love makes us *want* to do the things that honor Him.

It isn't a drudgery or duty to serve our God. It's all about love. His love for us moves us to love Him right back, and that shared love becomes the catalyst for our service. "We love, because He first loved us" (1 John 4:19), says the Bible. So the greatest thing isn't serving God. It's knowing how much He loves us. When we know that, we will discover a passion to serve Him rising up within us. It's a passion that comes from our love for Him. When you are serving God as an overflow of His love poured out in your heart, serving becomes the exact opposite of a job. It is a joy!

Christ Wants to Have First Place in Your Life

This statement sounds true at first glance, but closer examination will show that it can actually set you on a wrong course in your grace walk. Christ doesn't want to be first place in your life. He wants you to recognize Him as *all* of your life.

If Jesus Christ wants the first-place spot, what comes second? What about third place? What comes after that? The whole concept is absurd because it implies that our lives can be divided into compartments, with Jesus being one of those compartments.

To understand this point, think about your physical life for a moment. What would you think if I were to suggest that breathing should have first place in your life? What if somebody else said that having a heartbeat should be number one in your life? Maybe someone else could argue, "No, your circulatory system should come first, then breathing, then having a heartbeat."

It's a ridiculous discussion because your body is a whole, unified entity. You can't prioritize which is most important. Your physical health will give expression to every one of those actions in your body. They all work together as they express your normal state of health.

In the same way, our lives are indivisible when it comes to the effect of Christ's presence within us. We can't divide our lives into marriage, parenting, career, hobbies, and so on. All of those areas make up our lifestyle as one unified life, and Jesus is the source of our attitudes and actions in each of those areas.

The Truth Is So Much Better!

Jesus Christ isn't first place in your life. He *is* your life. He is the essence of who you are. Paul wrote in Colossians 3:4, "When Christ, who is our life, is revealed, then you also will be revealed with Him in glory." He described life in Philippians 1:21 by saying, "To me, to live is Christ and to die is gain."

Note that Paul didn't give Jesus a high place in his life. Paul realized that the very core of his existence was his union with Jesus Christ. He said it this way in Galatians 2:20: "I have been crucified with Christ; and it is no longer I who live, but Christ lives in me; and the life which I now live in the flesh I live by faith in the Son of God, who loved me and gave Himself up for me."

There it is. Paul said that he didn't have a life apart from Jesus Christ. That's true for you too. While it may sound admirable to say that we want Him to be number one in our lives, it misses the point of our union with Him altogether.

Christ wants to be recognized as the life of your family, career, hobbies, finances, and so on. Do you see the point? He is your everything!

Clarify Your Thinking

We do ourselves a disservice when we think that Jesus is a part of our lives, even if it is the number one part. He is the substance of everything that you are. He is our very essence.

You know you're on the right track in your thoughts when you find yourself seeing your marriage relationship as Christ living His life through you, expressing His love and life to your mate. Parenting becomes an expression of His life when we know that He is loving and guiding our children through us. You have a right understanding of priorities when you know He animates your activity at work.

When we know the truth, we stop thinking of Jesus holding first place in our lives and we begin thinking of Jesus being the source that animates every place in our lives. His isn't number one. He's the whole list!

God Wants to Give You What You Need

Does God really want to give us what we need in life? If so, here's the question that we have to answer: What do we lack right now? The truth is that we don't lack anything. We already have everything we need in Jesus Christ.

The nature of the flesh is to be insecure and fearful. When we look at ourselves to see if we measure up to the challenges of life, we will always conclude that we don't. We will see deficits in ourselves. We will become consumed with nagging fears about what we think we lack, and we will find ourselves asking God to give us those things.

The problem with that way of living is that it totally misses the point. We don't have to live that way. The idea that we don't have all that we need at this very moment is an illusion. It's a deception fostered upon our minds, causing us to feel as though God still has something left to give us, and we must have it.

The Truth Is So Much Better!

This underlying sense that we lack what we need is epidemic among many of us. People find themselves in an endless pursuit for something more because they don't realize that they already have what they need because of Christ. They run from conference to conference, book to book, preacher to preacher, trying to find that missing link. They want that new anointing or miraculous breakthrough that will blast their spiritual lives into orbit, where they can live successfully. It's always around the corner, in the next revival, at the upcoming seminar, or embedded in the newest spiritual wave from heaven.

It's a tragic viewpoint because it so contradicts what the Bible teaches. Paul described your provision in Ephesians 1:3. He wrote, "Blessed be the God and Father of our Lord Jesus Christ, who *has blessed us with every spiritual blessing* in the heavenly places in Christ."

Look carefully at that verse. How many spiritual blessings are provided in Christ? Will the experience Paul described in that verse happen one day, or has it already happened? The answer is clear. You are in Christ, and at this very moment, you have everything you need.

You may be thinking, "Wait a minute. That verse says *spiritual* blessings. What about the rest of life?" That kind of dualistic thinking is a curse to modern man. It implies that two worlds exist—one spiritual and the other natural—and they never intersect. Nothing could be further from the truth.

Your life in Christ is played out on the stage of this physical world. Because of His indwelling life, you don't lack anything. Nothing. You have all you need in Him right now. The apostle Peter affirmed the same:

> Grace and peace be multiplied to you in the knowledge of God and of Jesus our Lord; seeing that his divine power *has granted to us everything pertaining to life and godliness,* through the true knowledge of Him who called us by His own glory and excellence (2 Peter 1:2-3).

Note again that these have *already* been given to us. Because of what Jesus has done, we have received the whole supply from God the Father. In Him, nothing is left out.

Clarify Your Thinking

Don't make the mistake of thinking that you lack something necessary to live the lifestyle God intends for you to experience. He has deposited in you all that you need. The key to life isn't that you depend on Him to give you something else. You need to recognize that there's nothing left for Him to give you!

In Jesus Christ, you already have it all! We need to stop asking God to give us something and instead start accessing the benefits of what we already have in Him. Our intentions may be good, but our actions are misdirected when we ask Him to give us anything.

What do you need? Wisdom? That's Him. Peace? That's Him too. Strength? Him again. Power? Yes. Do you see the point? The apostle Paul said, "In Him all the fullness of Deity dwells in bodily form, in Him you have been made *complete*" (Colossians 2:9). Let's stop asking and start thanking Him for all He has given us. And most importantly, let's start living as though it's true.

Lie #14

We Need to Focus on Overcoming Our Sins

One could easily come to the conclusion that the most important subject among believers is sin based on the widespread popularity of the topic in popular Christian books, sermons, and Bible studies. Sin management often seems to be the reason for public ministry, and it appears to be the most important goal many who follow Jesus have embraced for their lives.

Overcoming sinful actions in life consumes the thoughts and energy of many sincere Christians. They are completely dedicated to stopping the wrong things they do and replacing them with actions that glorify God. Their motives are certainly pure, but their goal and focus is completely misguided.

Scripture does not call us to direct our attention toward our sins and exert our energy on eliminating them. In fact, this approach will not only be ineffective in reducing sinful actions but will also increase wrong behavior in our lifestyles. The Bible teaches that we shouldn't focus on sins at all. Instead, we should give Jesus Christ our undivided attention.

The Truth Is So Much Better!

The apostle Paul dealt with the subject of our focus by warning the churches he established in grace not to make sins their focus but to look to Christ instead. To the Colossian church, he wrote, "Set your mind on the things above, not on the things that are on the earth" (Colossians 3:2). He warned the Roman church, "The mind set on the flesh is death, but the mind set on the Spirit is life and peace" (Romans 8:6).

Trying to overcome sin by focusing on it has the exact opposite effect of what we want in our lives. If we fixate on what we do wrong and try to figure out how to conquer the bad behavior, we will always come up with some sort of plan that involves our own willpower and determination. When that happens, it doesn't matter how sincere we might be. We are setting ourselves up to fail. Taking an approach that contradicts what the Bible says about our sins won't work, despite the fact that we are sincere and even ask for God's help. He will not help us with *our* method. Instead, He will let us fail until we come to the place where we are willing to learn and accept *His* answer concerning our sinful actions.

Any approach we take in overcoming our own sins through self-discipline is legalistic because it stirs up within us the false hope that there is something *we* can do to defeat it. We don't have to conquer our sins. After all, Jesus Christ already has defeated sin. When we try to do what He has already accomplished, we are then denying the sufficiency of His grace and are attempting to utilize a legalistic method to do it ourselves. Legalistic methods doom us to failure. Paul wrote that "sinful passions…were *aroused* by the Law" (Romans 7:5). He warned the Corinthians who were trapped in sinful behavior that "the power of sin is the Law" (1 Corinthians 15:56).

Legalistic attempts to overcome sins by self-imposed rules and self-determination are to sins what gasoline is to flames. It won't stop them—it will only make matters worse. The only way to enjoy victory over sin is to rest in the victory that is already ours because of Christ's finished work. He defeated sin once and for all. Transformation comes to our lifestyle when we simply believe that reality and stop trying to do something that He has already done. We simply rest in His victory and direct our attention to Him. When we do that, the sins that have wielded power over us fall aside into impotency.

The author of Hebrews teaches us about the sufficiency of Christ's death in forever dealing with our sins:

> The Law, since it has only a shadow of the good things to come and not the very form of things, can never, by the same sacrifices which they offer continually year by year, make perfect those who draw near. Otherwise, would they not have ceased to be offered, because the worshipers, having once been cleansed, would no longer have had consciousness of sins? (Hebrews 10:1-3).

The writer of Hebrews points out that the Old Testament sacrifices of the priests were ineffective in perfectly freeing the people from their sins. If their sacrifices had worked, the passage tells us two things would have happened. First, they would have stopped offering them. With the sins of the people completely and permanently resolved, the priests would have had no need to keep offering the sacrifices.

Second, the Scripture tells us that if the people had indeed been permanently cleansed of their sins, they "would no longer have had consciousness of sins." Look at that statement in your own Bible, and let the implication of this verse settle into your understanding. The Bible says that *if* the Old Testament sacrifices had perfectly and permanently dealt with the sins of the people, *they would have stopped focusing on sins completely.* They would "no longer have…consciousness of sins." Why? It's because there would have been no need to focus on something that had been permanently and perfectly put away.

Those Old Testament sacrifices couldn't accomplish that, though, so the priests had to keep offering up their sacrifices again and again. Every year, they would offer the sacrifice on the Day of Atonement, and every year, the people would again be reminded of their sinfulness. It was "impossible for the blood of bull and goats to take away sins" (Hebrews 10:4).

Then, the Scripture points to Jesus in Hebrews 10. He came saying to the Father, "Behold, I have come to do Your will." What was the Father's will for His Son? "He takes away the first [covenant] in order to establish the second" (10:9).

That's exactly what Jesus did when He offered Himself as the perfect sacrifice for our sins. He dealt with every sin we would ever commit in our lifetimes and even crucified the old self, which caused us to want to sin in the first place (see Romans 6:6). He ended the old covenant, in which atoning for one's sins had to be done over and over and even being *conscious* of sins was necessary. Then He rolled out a new covenant, under which our sins would be put away and we would never have to focus on them again! The Old Testament priest's job was never finished, but when Jesus died, He cried out, "It is finished!"

The writer of Hebrews agrees:

> Every priest stands daily ministering and offering time after time the same sacrifices, which can never take away sins; but He [Jesus], having offered one sacrifice for sins for all time, *sat down at the right hand of God* (Hebrews 10:11-12).

Jesus did what no Old Testament sacrifice could do. He fully dealt with the matter of our sins so that we don't have to focus on them anymore. Then He sat down by the right hand of God, not because He was tired, but because *there is nothing left to do* when it comes to the matter of our sins.

Clarify Your Thinking

The lie that we need to focus on overcoming our sins is so very dangerous because it takes our eyes off Jesus Christ and puts them on our sins and an imaginary ability we think we have to solve the matter ourselves. If it seems to you as though I'm minimizing sin in this chapter, I ask you to consider this possibility: I'm not the one who is minimizing sin. Instead, the people who teach that we need to focus on overcoming our sins are the ones who minimize sins. Their teaching suggests that sin is so weak that it can be overcome by religious self-discipline.

Only one person could effectively deal with your sins, and He did—perfectly and completely. You don't have to tiptoe through life worried that you're going to step on a land mine of temptation and be destroyed by sin. You can run with carefree abandon through the fields of grace, knowing that your Father has swept the field for you already. It is His responsibility to see that you make it through life without being destroyed by sin.

If you fall down, He will pick you up, dust you off, and set you back on your course again. With assurance of that reality, you never have to focus on sins again. Just focus on Him, and as you do, you'll be amazed at the way sinful inclinations and temptations lose their power over you.

When I was a teen, we sang a chorus that suggested that if we simply turn our eyes upon Jesus and look intently into His wonderful face, all the things of earth—including the urge to commit sins—would grow strangely dim in the light of His glory and grace. Jesus Christ has defeated your sins. Let them go and focus your attention on Him. There's nothing else in life so worthy of your gaze or so effective in causing you to live your life the way God intends.

Lie #15

We Need to Continually Ask God to Forgive Our Sins

While we're on the subject of sins, let's consider another one that is closely related to the lie we examined in the last chapter. I wrote in the last chapter that we aren't to focus on our sins. Does that mean then that we aren't even to ask for forgiveness when we have sinned? The idea that we need to ask God to forgive our sins daily (or even more often) is so ingrained and taken for granted that people look at you as if you were an out-of-your-mind heretic for even questioning it. It is considered self-evident in the modern church. But it's not at all what the Bible teaches.

"Behold, the Lamb of God who takes away the sin of the world!" said John the Baptist (John 1:29). The Lamb of God came to do what? To take away the sin of the world. Did John really believe Jesus came to do that? Do you? Did He succeed?

The New Testament consistently teaches that Jesus Christ came to take away our sin. The root of this error is the fact that we really don't know—or don't accept—the testimony of the Scriptures. The Bible says that the problem of sin has been completely dealt with by Christ's death on the cross.

The Old Testament adds its own witness to this truth through much of its symbolism. One of the great pictures of Christ's accomplishment can be seen in the use of the scapegoat on the Day of Atonement. The scapegoat would be brought before the priest, and he would lay his hands on the head of the goat. By doing so, he would symbolically transfer the sins of the people to that goat. Then the goat would be driven away from the people and into the wilderness. It was a vivid picture, teaching that the sins of the people were carried away and would never return. That's exactly what Christ did with your sins and mine as "the Lamb of God." He took our sins away so that they're not an issue anymore.

The Truth Is So Much Better!

Following Jesus' death and resurrection, forgiveness of sins is announced as a done deal. Notice how Paul preached the gospel to a synagogue of people who were hearing of Christ for the first time: "Let it be known to you, brethren, that through Him *forgiveness of sins is proclaimed to you,* and through Him everyone who believes is freed from all things, from which you could not be freed through the Law of Moses" (Acts 13:38-39). Forgiveness of sins. That's the good news Paul told them about when he preached. Did he proclaim that their sins *could* be forgiven? No, the gospel is that their sins *were* forgiven, and their only need was to believe the good news! The potential for having their sins forgiven was present in the Old Testament sacrifices, but they could never be permanently freed under the Law of Moses. However, through Jesus Christ we can believe that we are forever freed from our sins because He is the perfect sacrifice.

Today, we are united with Christ, and we are now totally forgiven—not occasionally, not sometimes, not *if* we do something. Forgiveness is simply found in Him. Paul wrote, "*In Him we have* redemption through His blood, *the forgiveness of our trespasses,* according to the riches of His grace" (Ephesians 1:7). He told the Colossian church, "For He rescued us from the domain of darkness, and transferred us to the kingdom of His beloved Son, in whom we have redemption, *the forgiveness of sins*" (Colossians 1:13-14).

These are just a few examples of the New Testament's constant teaching. Why would people struggle to accept it? Mainly, it's because of two objections those who resist this good news typically raise. One is this petition from the Lord's Prayer: "Forgive us our debts, as we also have forgiven our debtors" (Matthew 6:12).

The answer to this objection is to take a look at the context of that prayer. Jesus taught this prayer before His own death and resurrection. That fact can't be stressed too much. When we study the Bible, it's not only important to consider what was said, but also *who* said it and *when* it was said. Context is everything in honest biblical understanding.

The Bible is clear that the new covenant didn't begin until the death of Jesus. So when Jesus spoke those words, which covenant was He speaking under? The old covenant, of course. It's important to recognize that while Jesus was full of grace in His dealings with people, His teaching existed within the context of the old covenant. If we fail to recognize that fact when we read the Scriptures, we will be filled with confusion about what He said at times.

One man asked me accusingly one day, "So you don't think we should do what Jesus plainly said?"

"Do *you* really believe we should do everything He said?" I asked him in return.

"Of course I do!" he answered impatiently. "His words are truth and life to me!"

"Okay," I responded, "can I ask you why you have two eyeballs in your skull?"

"What do you mean?" he asked.

"Well, in the Sermon on the Mount, Jesus said that if we've ever lusted, we should pluck our eyes out of our skull, and I've never met a man yet who hasn't lusted at some point in his life. Can you explain that to me?" I asked him as I pointed at his eyes.

The man became agitated with me and walked away. The point is that even this man—who vehemently argued that we must take all that Jesus said and apply those words to ourselves—personally realized that

Jesus said some things that don't apply now to those who live under the new covenant.

I believe we should take the words of Jesus seriously enough not only to know what He said, but also to consider whom He was talking to and what He meant by what He said. That's the case with the prayer He taught these old covenant saints to pray.

If you resist my view on this matter, I ask you this question: Do *you* take with equal seriousness the insistence to apply everything He said to yourself? In the same context where Jesus taught the disciples the "model prayer," He also talked about how that if you don't forgive others, God won't forgive you. Do you apply that one to your life personally too? Based on that statement, anybody who remains unforgiving toward someone else is not forgiven by God at this very moment. They would be in danger of hell itself if they were to die in that state. I wonder how many people who have trusted Christ and profess to be forgiven by Him are withholding any degree of forgiveness toward any other person in the world. It's food for thought, to say the least. We'd better hope we're completely forgiven now (and we are), or a lot of people who profess to be believers are in reality in deep trouble.

The second major objection about the complete forgiveness truth comes from the way many people understand 1 John 1:9: "If we confess our sins, He is faithful and righteous to forgive us our sins and to cleanse us from all unrighteousness."

Let's begin with an elementary and obvious fact. If you believe that this verse teaches you have to continually ask God to forgive your sins, then you are interpreting that verse in a way that contradicts what all of the rest of the New Testament has to say. There are dozens of verses that *clearly* teach the results of Christ's finished work on the cross, and how we are forgiven. Would we argue that one verse in 1 John stands as an authority in contradiction to all those verses?

We don't build our belief system around one verse that may *seem* to stand in contrast to other verses. If something appears to be a contradiction, we should go back and look more carefully at the meaning of that verse. That's very important here.

There is a clear answer that explains the confusion about 1 John 1:9. John was writing to a church containing both believers and unbelievers. False teachers who were bringing ideas contradictory to our faith were also infiltrating this church. They were later known as the Gnostics, people who were confusing the Christians about what constituted sin among them.

John indicates the problem when he writes, "These things I have written to you concerning those who are trying to deceive you" (1 John 2:26). There were some weak believers there who were becoming confused about the whole matter. Much of this letter is meant to give those believers criteria to identify who was teaching the truth and who wasn't.

Clarify Your Thinking

What does it all mean then? Do we just ignore the times we sin? Am I suggesting that sin doesn't matter? Of course not! It's the nature of the person who follows Jesus to acknowledge when we sin. The important thing is to realize that when we do, we should admit it before the Lord. We don't do it in order to be forgiven. We do it because we *have been* forgiven.

Don't get bogged down in a faulty understanding of 1 John 1:9 when the rest of the New Testament teaches that our sins have been absolutely forgiven—past, present, and future. It's amazing how many people who balk at the idea that we don't have to keep asking for forgiveness cling to 1 John 1:9 while ignoring every other verse in the New Testament that clearly says all our sins have already been forgiven. Confessing your sins will bring an *experiential awareness* of forgiveness, but it isn't confession that brings forgiveness. The work of Jesus Christ on the cross did that!

If you believe you have to constantly ask God to forgive your sins, you're believing a lie that will keep you in bondage. You will be sin-conscious all the time. But if you believe what the New Testament teaches—that all of your sins have been wiped out and carried away by the finished work of Christ—you will live focused on Jesus Christ, and the truth that you are already 100 percent totally forgiven. And *that* is a truth that will set you free!

Lie #16

When We Do Wrong, We Are out of Fellowship with God

O ut of fellowship with God." It's a phrase you hear Christians say a lot. But what does that really mean? Does it mean that we and God are at odds with each other? Or that somehow there's a strain or distance between us? The word *fellowship* is not often used outside of church buildings these days, but it's a biblical word. It means "closeness, unity with one another, oneness." That seems to make reasonable sense.

I have one question, though, to show you the problem. How can you be separated or have distance from someone who lives *in you?*

The idea that we're out of fellowship with God when we do wrong is a lie. It's one of those clichés. It sounds good, but it's not biblical. There is nothing you can do to put yourself out of fellowship with God.

Certainly, when we have sinned, whenever we've done wrong, our *perception* of that fellowship is radically changed. The situation is illustrated well in the story of the prodigal son in Luke 15. When this young prodigal went off into the far country, what was the attitude of the father? Did he stop loving his son? Was he angry with him? Did he feel differently about him? Not at all. There is nothing in the biblical account to even hint at that possibility.

While this son was in rebellion, he certainly forfeited the experiential privileges of being a son. Back home, the father only grieved for the son's loss, saddened by his son's foolish choices. He hated to see his boy hurt himself that way, but his love and acceptance of the son never wavered in the least.

Had anything changed with the father? Nothing had. However, the son's perception of fellowship had been radically changed when he was in the pigpen. He thought he was now estranged from his father, as evidenced by how he concocted a story about how he planned to go back. He was going to go home and say, "I've sinned against heaven and in your sight. I'm no longer worthy to be your son. Make me as a servant. I'll do better."

But when he got home, the father never even let him give the speech. The father ran to meet him and threw his arms around him. His love was overflowing in a way that fathers simply didn't express in that ancient Near Eastern culture. It was considered undignified for a man to pull up his cloak, bare his legs and run with laughter and passion like this man did. But he didn't care. He was thrilled to see his child abandon his foolishness and come back home to enjoy his place as a son. Jesus was describing the loving acceptance of God the Father toward His foolish children, some of whom go off into a bad place and then wrongly think their Father's attitude toward them has changed.

From the father's perspective, he had always been in fellowship with his son. The son simply had not been able to enjoy that fellowship. And that's how it is with you and with me. Your Father's heart toward you never changes. When we do wrong, are we out of fellowship with Him? Only in our own distorted thinking. The reality is that we're always in oneness with Him. You can't get any closer than that.

The Truth Is So Much Better!

The apostle John wrote, "This is the message we have heard from Him and announced to you, that God is Light, and in Him there is no darkness at all. If we say that we have fellowship with Him and yet walk in the darkness, we lie and do not practice the truth" (1 John 1:5-6).

God is Light. You are in God. So you are in the light. You can't walk in darkness because God is Light, and in Him is no darkness at all. It may look dark to you because sins blind you to the light, but you're still there nonetheless. To say you are "in the dark" or "out of fellowship" with your Father is to not practice (live) the truth.

John goes on to say, "But if we walk in the Light as He Himself is in the Light, we have fellowship with one another, and the blood of Jesus His Son cleanses us from all sin" (1 John 1:7). If you practice the truth by realizing that you are walking in the light of His grace at every moment, *you will know* by first-hand experience what it means to live in fellowship together with your Father and what it means to continuously be kept completely cleansed from all sin by the blood of Jesus! It's true whether we know it or not, but what a joy it is to *know* that we are in fellowship with God and are cleansed of all sin!

The word "fellowship" is the Greek word *koinonia*. It means "association, communion, joint participation." The association you have with your Father isn't determined by your behavior, but by His grace. At times you may *feel* like you are "out of fellowship," but you are not.

Clarify Your Thinking

Fellowship is not about our feelings. It's about how we're related to God because of the finished work of Jesus Christ. You see it in Paul's opening remarks to the church at Corinth, a group that he would have to spend the better part of three years correcting because they were misbehaving in so many ways.

Beginning his first letter to them, he writes, "God is faithful, through whom you were called into fellowship with His Son, Jesus Christ our Lord" (1 Corinthians 1:9). They weren't in fellowship with God because they were doing the right things. They were in fellowship with God because God called them into fellowship with His Son, and He is faithful to us even when we mess up in life. He is the One who sees to it that nothing changes. Any change we may imagine is only in our darkened understanding at the time. We can live *in the light* and be blind to the reality of that light, but it doesn't change the truth.

You are in fellowship with God all the time. Your perception of that may change, but remember: Your feelings are not the standard of truth. The promises of God in Holy Scripture are. I assure you: The idea that we're out of fellowship with God when we do wrong is a lie. Your Father is in fellowship with you *all* the time, and when we understand that truth, it causes us to want to live a lifestyle that glorifies Him.

You Should Live by the Teachings of the Bible

Here's a lie that might well cause you trouble if you even dare to question its accuracy among most Christians. To suggest that we aren't to live by the Bible sounds ludicrous—if not downright heretical—to many who have been taught all their lives that the Bible was written precisely to show us how we are supposed to live.

To consider this matter, let's go back to a fundamental question: Was the Bible written as a guidebook that is intended to show us how to live? Is that its purpose? I don't think so. There is no doubt that the Bible is profitable for instruction in righteousness. It makes that claim for itself (see 2 Timothy 3:16-17). But this is the question: "What does it mean to be instructed in righteousness?" Is it a matter of learning how we are supposed to act? Is that what the instruction is all about for us? To learn how to behave? No, it is not.

What does it mean to be righteous? We can be sure of several things because of what the Bible plainly says about that question. First, we know that righteousness is a gift that comes to us in Christ. It's not something we achieve by anything we do. Romans 5:17 says that because of the abundance of God's grace, we have received the *gift* of righteousness. What is the gift of righteousness that is ours? First Corinthians 1:30 teaches us that Christ Himself is our righteousness. Paul wrote, "By His doing you are in Christ Jesus, who became to us...righteousness." *He* is our righteousness. Our righteousness isn't based at all on what we do, but on what He has done.

The Bible instructs us about righteousness, and righteousness is a person—not a religious performance we carry out. When we understand this, we will clearly see that the Bible is intended to point us to Jesus Christ. It instructs us about Him! The Bible is all about Him and who He is. It's about what He has done on our behalf. It's about His love for us. Once again—it's not about *us* and what we're supposed to do!

So we aren't to live by the teachings of the Bible. We are to live by the life of the Christ who indwells us! The Bible teaches us more about Him and what it means that we live in union with Him. Our actions flow out of that knowledge, not out of some moral code we wrongly try to draw from Scripture.

The Truth Is So Much Better!

Some might argue that this view diminishes the role of Scripture in our lives, but I strongly disagree. To the contrary, when we turn the Bible into a guidebook that gives religious and moral instruction as opposed to a picture album that reveals the beauty of Jesus Christ to us, *that* faulty viewpoint undermines the very essence of the Bible. Many books out there can offer moral guidelines for living, but only one book reveals Jesus Christ in His glory and beauty the way Scripture does— and that book is our Holy Bible! Don't diminish the Bible's value by trying to live by its teachings. Hold the Bible in high esteem by recognizing that it is our Father's message to us, showing us Jesus and enabling us to see what it looks like when He expresses Himself through our lifestyles each day.

If you've been taught that the primary value of the Bible is its teaching about how you should live, you're not in the minority. Even in Jesus' day, there were those who thought the Scripture was given as a rule-book intended to guide our behavior.

To first-century Jews, the most upright religious people in the world were the Pharisees. They were experts on the Bible. They were biblical intellectuals, the moral leaders of their nation, and the most dedicated and self-disciplined religious practitioners around. If you want to find somebody who tried with all their hearts to live by the teachings of the Bible, you have to look no further than the Pharisees. They knew their Bibles, the Old Testament Scriptures, like the back of their hand. However, according to Jesus, they missed the whole point of their Bibles.

Jesus said to them, "You search the Scriptures because you think that in them you have eternal life; *it is these that testify about Me; and you are unwilling to come to Me* so that you may have life" (John 5:39-40). They had their Bibles in hand and studied them much. In fact, they could quote most of the Old Testament, but Jesus said they simply didn't get it. While they professed to be focused on living by the teaching of their Bibles, Jesus said they were missing Him.

Clarify Your Thinking

There are Christians today who talk more about the Bible than they do Jesus. That should be a red flag. The Bible is not an end unto itself. Nor is it a guidebook or a handbook for living. The Bible is a grace book that points us to Jesus Christ. He is the end that we pursue. If we are not led to the person of Christ and to faith in Him, like the Pharisees, we are missing the whole point of the Bible.

I realize this viewpoint may be uncomfortable for some people. It may sound to you like I'm minimizing the place of the Bible in our lives, but I certainly hope not. Remember, this is coming from somebody who has spent his life studying, emphasizing, and teaching the Bible! I love the Bible more than I have words to express. But it's a paradox. As much as I love studying the Bible, and as much as I love teaching it and helping other people discover how great a blessing it is, learning the Bible is not the main thing.

As we live in Him and He lives through us, we will approach the Bible in the right way, knowing that Christ is our life source, and the Bible points us to Him. Through the Scriptures, Christ the living Word will reveal Himself to us, teaching us how He will live his life through us. We absolutely love our Bibles, but we live by the life of Jesus Christ.

Lie #18

You Need to Find God's Perfect Will for Your Life

Finding and fulfilling God's will for your life is one of the greatest mandates laid on us by the modern church world. We *must* find God's perfect will. After all, you wouldn't want to miss His will for your life, would you? It all sounds so good, so noble. What pursuit could be better than trying to find God's will for our lives? There's just one thing wrong with that popular belief. It's not biblical. Nowhere does the Scripture tell us that the will of God is something that we have to find.

Are you beginning to see that these lies we are identifying seem to have a common denominator? Almost all of them point toward things *you* must do in your walk with God. They are pregnant with a heavy sense of "you ought to," "you need to," or "you should." This perspective that puts the responsibility on you is the underlying foundation of legalism. It's all about what you do instead of what our loving Father has already done.

To insist that you need to find God's perfect will for your life clearly puts the burden on you to find something that's not apparent to you. Multitudes of sermons have been preached through the years giving the roadmap for finding the will of God. The problem is that when we follow those religious maps, we discover they only lead to uncertainty and frustration.

I have met countless people who have nearly driven themselves to desperation trying to find the perfect answer about God's will for their lives. Many Christians live in almost neurotic fear that they have missed it (or will miss it in the future). They live in terrible self-doubt about past choices, racking their brains in self-analysis: "Did I marry the right person? Did I marry the wrong person? Did I go to the right college? Did I go into the right profession? Am I working at the right company? Living in the right town?" They are paralyzed in their present decision-making in the same kind of self-doubt.

Consider this: How *could* someone discover the answer to such questions? God doesn't normally speak in an audible voice. He hasn't written a message on a wall in a long time (as far as I know, the last time was in 539 B.C. in a story recorded in the book of Daniel). It's no wonder that under such pressure people will resort to techniques that often border on absolute superstition in their attempt to try to find the answers.

That's not grace, and it's certainly not truth. That is legalism at its core. The truth is, you don't need to find God's will for your life. God will make His will known to you through your relationship with Christ. In fact, the will of God for your life *is* Jesus Christ. He is your life, and the Father's will for your life will be made known to you through the walk you have with His Son. You won't have to find it. He will show it to you.

The Truth Is So Much Better!

There is no place in the New Testament that calls on believers to seek to discover the perfect will of God for our lives. It's just not there. Look as long as you like, and you'll not find a passage that says such a thing.

Do the Scriptures have anything at all to say about the subject? Yes. Paul talked about knowing God's will in Romans 12:1. He wrote, "Therefore I urge you, brethren, by the mercies of God, to present your bodies a living and holy sacrifice, acceptable to God, which is your spiritual service of worship."

Note that this is essentially the second command to action Paul makes in the book of Romans (the first one is a brief, similar exhortation in 6:11-14). He has spent 11 chapters teaching us about the grace of God in Jesus Christ before he turns to urge us what to do about it. That should tell us something about the Christian life. Everything we are told to *do* should be built on the understanding that forms the foundation of those choices. We have put way too much behavioral teaching on the shoulders of people who have an inadequate understanding of who Jesus Christ is in them—and who they are in Him.

So what is Paul's first command to action? Based on who Jesus is and what He's done (that's what Paul means by "the mercies of God"), we are to give ourselves to Him wholeheartedly in the spirit of worshipful submission—the recognition of the fact that God *is* God and we aren't. That's it. It may sound simple, but that's the way grace is. We recognize who He is and who we are. That's a huge step in the right direction. Yield yourself completely to Him.

Then having made this first fundamental choice, Paul adds, "And do not be conformed to this world, but be transformed by the renewing of your mind, so that you may prove what the will of God is, that which is good and acceptable and perfect" (Romans 12:2).

Paul says it's very simple, really, to discern God's will for your life. You just present yourself to Him and trust Him to show you what it is. You choose not to be conformed to the way the world thinks. A worldly approach says, "If it's going to be, it's up to me," but that's not the way your Father has planned it. We are to submit to Him as the standard of truth, not the culture around us or to other people's opinions.

Clarify Your Thinking

The lie is that you have to go find God's will, as if it's hidden from you. The truth is that it is God's responsibility to make His will known to you and then see that it's carried out through you. You don't have to find it. It is revealed. Let your focus be Jesus Christ. As you focus on Him, the will of God for you will be made manifest. You don't have to be filled with anxiety over missing God's will, because it's not up to you to keep yourself in the center of God's will. It's God's responsibility to do that. That's why it's called grace. And He will do exactly that. Don't worry that you'll get out of the will of God. He'll take care of things.

God has a calling (a plan) for you, and He will ensure that you know it and do it. The Bible says that He is faithful not only to make His calling known to you, but also to bring it to pass in your life (see 1 Thessalonians 5:24).

So don't accept the lie that you have to find God's will. It isn't necessary for you to take on such pressure. You weren't intended to carry that responsibility. That's His role. What is our response to be? "In everything give thanks; for *this is God's will for you* in Christ Jesus" (1 Thessalonians 5:18). Just relax, yield yourself to Him, and know He'll make it happen in His time and in His way. The only thing left for us to do is to say, "Thank You!" *That* is His will for you.

God Is Disappointed in You When You Do Wrong

This lie is constantly used in the modern church world to motivate and manipulate people to straighten up and act right. It's a guilt-trip ticket passed out by many in religious authority to anybody who is willing to take it. I'm not proud to admit that I've dispensed this ticket to self-condemnation at times to members of congregations I served, to counselees, to friends, and even to my family.

To suggest to people that God is disappointed in them is a guilt-and-shame technique straight from the enemy of our souls. He uses this lie against us to keep us wallowing in self-condemnation. For too many years, I used to teach, "Don't disappoint God!" "Do the things He expects you to do!" "Live up to what He requires of you so that He won't be disappointed in you." I could manipulate an outward response from people with that kind of teaching, but it didn't accomplish the goal our Father has in mind, which is for us to rest in His love. I know now that it only served to cause people to feel ashamed, like they didn't measure up to what God had expected of them.

We may talk about disappointing God, but the truth of the Scripture is this: *It is impossible for you to disappoint God.* Not only is the idea we can disappoint God a lie—it's impossible.

Think about the idea of disappointment for a moment. Disappointment is the result of an unfulfilled or unrealized expectation. To be disappointed means that a person expects that an outcome will be one thing, when in fact it turns out in a different way. So to suggest that God could be disappointed implies that God doesn't know everything. It suggests that He's waiting to see how things are going to turn out and hoping it will go the way He wants. With only a moment's thought, you know that can't be right. God doesn't hope anything. He already knows everything in advance. That means it's impossible for Him to be disappointed.

Knowing everything we would do in life, including all the wrong, He dealt with it for us before we even showed up on the earth. When Jesus took your sin into Himself on the cross, He saw clearly every sin you would ever commit. He saw all your sins of omission and commission. He knew exactly what you would and wouldn't do throughout your entire lifetime, and He absorbed it all into Himself, doing away with it forever. So if God already knows everything you're going to do in your lifetime, nothing is a surprise to Him. We might be disappointed in ourselves, but God can never be disappointed in us.

The Truth Is So Much Better!

What does God expect us to do? The answer may surprise you: Nothing! Why? Because God realizes we're incapable of doing anything on our own. The Scripture says no flesh will "glory in his sight" (1 Corinthians 1:29 KJV). That is, no human beings will ever be able to brag about their accomplishments before God.

That's a biblical fact that slams human pride. "Don't you think," people ask in exasperation, "that, at the least, God expects us to do the right thing?" It's important for us to be crystal clear about one thing. That question implies that the main concern God has for you is that you live a moral life—and nothing could be further from the truth. That's the big thing in religion, but it's not what God is focused on at all. Your Father wants you to *know* Him in intimacy. That's the very essence of salvation (see John 17:3). When that happens, every action of our lifestyles will find expression from that knowledge.

Our role is to simply live our lives with the confident assurance that it is He who animates our behavior. That's the pattern Jesus described in His metaphor of the vine and branches. He said, "I am the true vine, and My Father is the vinedresser...Abide in Me, and I in you. As the branch cannot bear fruit of itself unless it abides in the vine, so neither can you unless you abide in Me" (John 15:1,4).

Doesn't that make perfect sense? A disconnected branch has no ability to produce life or fruit. So the answer for the branch is in remaining attached to the source and allowing the life of the vine to flow through it. That's when fruit results. So it is with us. Because we're connected to Him, He will be the One who gives expression to our behavior as we depend on Him.

There's nothing we can do on our own. Jesus went on to say, "I am the vine, you are the branches; he who abides in Me and I in him, he bears much fruit, for apart from Me you can do nothing" (John 15:5). So when we *try* to live what many call "the Christian life," we are destined to fail. We will be disappointed with ourselves, but our Father knew all along what would happen.

Clarify Your Thinking

You don't have to walk around with guilt or fear that you have disappointed God. He wants your focus elsewhere. He wants you looking at Him, not looking at yourself in self-condemnation over your actions. Do our actions matter to Him? Of course they do. He loves us and doesn't want to see us make choices that hurt us. When we sin, we are disappointed, but His heart toward us is to rush to us in love and free us from the very thing that robs us of experiencing the complete joy of being His child.

Remember the story of the prodigal son in Luke 15? There we see the heart of our Father reflected in the prodigal's father. When the son came home from the pigpen, all covered with filth and the stench of the places he had been based on the foolish choices he had made, he must have felt very disappointed in himself. But the Bible tells us that when the father saw his son, he ran to him and fell on him in a loving embrace and gave him a heartfelt kiss.

What was the first thing the father said when he spoke upon the son's return? Do you remember? Here's what he said, speaking to his servants: "Quickly bring out the best robe and put it on him, and put a ring on his hand and sandals on his feet" (Luke 15:22).

Before the son could even give his prepared speech about how he had disappointed his father by his failures, the father cried out to his servants, "Get this boy cleaned up! My son is home. Wash the filth off him and put on him the best clothes money can buy. My boy is home! My boy is home! Let's have a party!"

Sound like a disappointed dad to you? Not to me. This sounds like a dad whose only concern was that his son enjoys the benefits of the dad's love and generosity. The son may have been disappointed, but the dad expressed no disappointment at all. His actions showed nothing but relief that his son had turned from those foolish choices and would now live in the luxurious benefits of his sonship.

That dad's attitude is a pale comparison of the heart of your heavenly Father toward you. He isn't disappointed with you. So don't wallow in the pigpen of shame anymore. Fall into His arms and let the party begin.

Lie #20

God Won't Put More on You Than You Can Bear

Perhaps nothing that one Christian says to another has been spoken with greater heartfelt sincerity that this statement: "God won't put more on you than you can bear." From the time I was a small child, I've heard this said in and outside of church. It's one of those sayings that seems like a self-evident truth because we've heard it so many times. Given the fact that our God is a loving Father, it seems to make perfect sense too.

Many Christians would immediately suggest that the teaching that God won't put more on you than you can bear is in the Bible, but actually the Bible teaches something very different. Generally, when people think this idea is biblical, their minds go to 1 Corinthians 10:13. That verse says, "No temptation has overtaken you but such as is common to man; and God is faithful, who will not allow you to be tempted beyond what you are able, but with the temptation will provide the way of escape also, so that you will be able to endure it."

That verse is a great one because it tells us that God won't allow us to be tempted beyond what we can endure. But the lie I'm addressing in this chapter isn't about temptation to sin. It's about the idea that God won't allow us to have *burdens* beyond our ability to endure. It's important to make the distinction between temptation to sin, and trials. This verse in 1 Corinthians 10:13 means God won't allow us to be tempted *to sin* beyond what we can bear, based on the strength of the indwelling Christ who lives in us.

Troubles and trials in life are another matter. Will God allow life's circumstances to be more than our human strength and ability can handle? If I were to tell you that He would, you may doubt or even deny my view, but would you agree that the apostle Paul is a trustworthy source of authority on the matter? Let's consider what he says on the subject.

The Truth Is So Much Better!

In regard to his circumstances, Paul relates a story of a time he clearly felt that his burdens were beyond his ability to handle. Note carefully what he said: "For we do not want you to be unaware, brethren, of our affliction which came to us in Asia, that we were burdened excessively, *beyond our strength,* so that we despaired even of life" (2 Corinthians 1:8).

Recognize that he said, "We were burdened excessively, beyond our strength." And remember, this is the great apostle—arguably the most effective Christian who has ever lived! Sometimes, we tend to put our biblical heroes up on pedestals, and we quickly forget that they were men and women who had experiences and feelings just like us. Their pain hurt just as much as ours does; their fears were as vivid as ours are; and they had to apply faith and courage just as we do.

Now I want to zero in on the phrase "beyond our strength." The New International Version of the Bible says it the best. The NIV renders the Greek words Paul used as "beyond our ability to endure." Do you see it? That's not simply an opinion I have that I'm trying to convince you to believe. This is the apostle Paul speaking. He said he and his companions "were under great pressure, *far beyond our ability to endure.*" In other words, for Paul, the pressure was "more than he could bear." Isn't it interesting how the Bible can correct faulty beliefs we may have held for a long time?

The question that immediately comes to mind may be, "If God does allow us to have burdens greater than we can bear, why would He do that?" After all, He loves us passionately, so what possible good reason could there be in Him allowing such a thing? The apostle Paul continues and answers that question: "Indeed, we had the sentence of death within ourselves *so that we would not trust in ourselves, but in God* who raises the dead" (2 Corinthians 1:9).

There you can see the good God is accomplishing by allowing us to face trials that are too much for us. He uses our burdens to teach us to put our total trust in Him and His power and to stop trying to handle life on our own. Then when He acts to either resolve the situation or to pour out His supernatural peace in our hearts, it will be absolutely clear who is the source of the victory. And we learn in a deeper way to trust the Lord with our lives and circumstances.

Clarify Your Thinking

To say that God will not put a burden on you greater than you can bear is a lie. To believe that may force you into a corner, where you'll feel like you have to act like you're doing okay when you're not feeling that way at all. So many Christians pretend that their burdens are nothing at all when they're with other people. But in their heart of hearts, they wonder why—if God truly loves them—their burdens aren't being lifted.

People reach ridiculous and damaging conclusions because of this type of confusion. Some have been made to feel like the fact that their burdens are weighing them down emotionally must mean that they don't have enough faith. Some think they must have hidden sin in their lives. Some think they have to fake it and act like everything is okay while they call their pretentious facade "faith."

Don't fall for this lie. Know that although your Father may at times allow you to experience a burden greater than your ability to endure, *He will carry it for you.* In fact, He will carry you. When we feel like we can't go on, the key is to cast our cares on Him. After all, He loves us and will sustain us until the crisis passes. In the meantime, we can rest in His arms. We can know that there's nothing wrong with our faith, commitment to Him, or His love for us. It's life, and life sometimes hurts unbearably. But even when it does, He is there with us to hold us and see that we pass safely through the hard times.

Lie #21

There Are Secular and Sacred Things in Life

One of the most damaging errors most people make is making a dualistic distinction between secular and sacred things in life. This way of seeing the world forces a separation where none is warranted. Most of all, people who believe this lie think that faith is contained in the "religious" part of our lives, and they assume that everything else has nothing to do with their Christian faith.

What comes to mind when you hear the word *sacred*? Many people would immediately think of church buildings, Bibles, clergymen, and everything else that could be considered religious. For them, the word *secular* encompasses everything else in life, which would basically be 95 percent of how people spend their lives and energy. This is how this mind-set operates: Church life is sacred, but work life is secular. Our prayer life is sacred, but our entertainment choices are secular. On and on the list could go. It's an artificial distinction we may make, but it's not true. And neither is it healthy.

This distinction has no basis in Scripture whatsoever. It is false, and it reveals a deep misunderstanding of the nature of the life we have in Jesus Christ. We don't have two lives—a "spiritual" life here and a "regular" life there. Our life in Christ is one unified lifestyle, and it is who we are wherever we are. It may surprise you to know that you don't move in and out of secular and sacred arenas in your lifestyle. It's all sacred.

The original meaning of the word *sacred* denotes the idea of something that is set apart for uncommon use in contrast to the word *secular*, which refers to the common things of everyday life. Utensils in the Old Testament temple were sacred because they weren't commonly used every day. They were uncommon because of their specialized use in the temple.

In the New Testament, Jesus often took common things and set them apart as sacred. When He declared it to be so, suddenly a common field ready to be harvested became a sacred field that proclaimed a message about the need for workers in the Father's harvest. Broken bread and blessed wine became sacred expressions of His very life, given for mankind. Anything He designates for Himself is sacred. That's true with human beings too. Today we refer to Saint Paul, Saint Peter, and many others in that way because we recognize how they were elevated to become the disciples and apostles of Jesus Christ.

We need to understand that this distinction doesn't just apply to people in the Bible. It's true of you too. You have been set apart by your Father, and He has put His own life into you. That makes *you* sacred! God Himself has created you as a divine work of art (see Ephesians 2:10). Jesus Christ lives in you, and you are an instrument through which He expresses His life and love. Because He is in you, you take Him everywhere you go. That fact has remarkable implications.

The Truth Is So Much Better!

Remember, we are *in* Him, and that is always true. Jesus Christ continually engulfs your life just like the air that sustains you physically. Where you are, He is. When you go to church, He's in you. When you go to work, He's in you. Even if you were to go to a place not compatible with the righteous nature you have in Him, He would still be in you.

The Bible teaches that you have been *sanctified.* The word suggests that you have been miraculously made holy by virtue of the fact that He has set you apart for Himself. You are a container and conduit of the very life of Jesus Christ. You take holiness with you everywhere you go; therefore, you sanctify your environment because of Him.

Scripture describes a situation in which a believing wife is married to a man who doesn't yet believe in Christ. The apostle Paul said that the "unbelieving husband is *sanctified* through his wife" (1 Corinthians 7:14). In other words, he's a marked man, marked by God Himself, just as the wife is. And in time, he will come to believe it. Many husbands have believed in Christ because of the godly influence of a believing wife.

Clarify Your Thinking

Because the Holy Spirit of Christ is in you, your environment is an uncommon, sacred environment. You don't have to concern yourself about being contaminated by this world's culture. Jesus didn't fear what some would call "the secular world." In fact, He plunged headfirst into it. By His presence in those environments, He made sacred those things considered secular.

The same is true today. Because you're in Christ, everything about your life is sacred. Our role as believers is to allow "Christ in us" to move into every sphere of our lives, bringing His influence to homes, families, businesses, governments—even churches. You don't live in a defensive mode. You have every reason to invade this world and know with confidence that the very gates of hell cannot prevail against the Christ who is in you.

We Need Revival

We who grew up in the evangelical world are familiar with the ongoing emphasis on the need for revival in the church. If we take the word of many spiritual leaders, we would think that revival is the cure-all for every need in the church. This idea may sound completely sensible, but it's not at all biblical.

Did you know that the word *revival* isn't even mentioned in the New Testament? I know that there are truths that aren't specifically mentioned by name in the Bible but are true nonetheless. For instance, the word *Trinity* isn't in the Bible, but we all know it is a biblical teaching. The word itself is not found in Scripture, but the concept clearly is.

That's not the case with revival, though. The New Testament gives no teaching at all on this subject. That should at least cause you to pause. The only biblical material on the subject of revival comes from the Old Testament. There's a reason for that. Revival is an old covenant concept. Read the Old Testament, and you will find that periodically through the centuries before Christ, Israel would return to the Lord after a long period of total unfaithfulness and idolatry. That was the meaning of revival. Her weakening life in faith would be newly invigorated—revived. When an individual would use this word, he usually meant that he was tired and discouraged and wanted the Lord to give him strength once again.

What people today mean by *revival* can vary. There have been times in church history where the Holy Spirit did something very unusual, something you can't bring about by human means. The Great Awakening in the eighteenth century is one famous example. But even eyewitnesses who led the movement couldn't explain what was happening. It certainly isn't repeatable by any human process.

Many Christians use the word *revival* to refer to a special week of worship services at their church with a guest speaker. The hope is for a spiritual "high" with many "decisions for Christ." Because the vast majority of those attending are already believers, those "decisions" would be called "rededications." People who make these decisions see themselves as having fallen short in their walk with the Lord, so they are now rededicating themselves with new zeal and commitment.

Many of us have been a part of this religious cultural phenomenon. These revivals come and go. When I was a boy, we would have revival services in the church twice a year. Make no mistake about it: When we experienced that revival—the renewed zeal and enthusiasm for the Lord—we felt encouraged. But we had to have revival every year (or even twice a year) because it faded away. That's why it's common in such churches to see the same people "rededicating" their lives every year. The Old Testament solution of revival is not the answer for New Testament believers.

The Truth Is So Much Better!

We need something better than revival—we need a *revelation*. That's why the New Testament doesn't talk about revival. Instead, it often reminds us of what we already have in Christ. Paul didn't pray for revival in the church. He asked for revelation:

> I too, having heard of the faith in the Lord Jesus which

exists among you and your love for all the saints, do not cease giving thanks for you, while making mention of you in my prayers; that the God of our Lord Jesus Christ, the Father of glory, *may give to you a spirit of wisdom and of revelation in the knowledge of Him* (Ephesians 1:15-17).

Do you see what Paul is praying for the Ephesians, and what he would have prayed for you? Not that you would experience a revival, but that God would open your mind to understand and know Him. This clearly is more than an emotional boost accompanied by renewed determination to follow Christ. Paul prayed that the church would have an understanding—a revelation—of something that had much greater potential than a short-lived revival. What did Paul want believers to understand?

I pray *that the eyes of your heart may be enlightened,* so that you will know what is the hope of His calling, what are the riches of the glory of His inheritance in the saints, and what is the surpassing greatness of His power toward us who believe (Ephesians 1:18-19).

He wanted the light to come on in the people's hearts so that they would know the benefits of having been called by the Father. He wanted them to know the wealth of provision that is our birthright in Christ. He prayed for them to grasp what it meant to possess the very power of the living Christ indwelling them. That revelation will do much more than temporarily motivate us. It will permanently transform us!

Revivals come and go. They get people excited, and then they fade away. In saying this, I understand that many people first began to follow Christ during "revival meetings," and He has touched many believers in those settings. God can work in any environment. But still, something better removes the need for periodic revivals—the revelation of who you are in Jesus Christ. I promise you: That will never grow old. It will never fade away.

In 2 Corinthians 3:7-11, Paul shows the difference between the new covenant concept of revelation and the old covenant idea of revival:

> But if the ministry of death, in letters engraved on stones, came with glory, so that the sons of Israel could not look intently at the face of Moses because of the glory of his face, fading as it was, how will the ministry of the Spirit fail to be even more with glory? For if the ministry of condemnation has glory, much more does the ministry of righteousness abound in glory. For indeed what had glory, in this case has no glory because of the glory that surpasses it. For if that which fades away was with glory, much more that which remains is in glory.

Paul is comparing the glory of the old covenant with the glory of the new covenant. There's no doubt that when Moses encountered God on Mount Sinai, his face radiated with reflected glory. There's no doubt about it—he was revived on that mountain. But the problem was that it immediately began to fade away. Yes, the old covenant revivals had a measure of glory, but nothing compared to the glory that we understand in the new covenant. When we receive this revelation of grace, this revelation of who we are in Christ, there is a new covenant glory that never fades away. It will never wear off. It won't need to be repeated.

Paul concludes the discussion saying, "But we all, with unveiled face, beholding as in a mirror the glory of the Lord, are being transformed into the same image from glory to glory, just as from the Lord, the Spirit" (2 Corinthians 3:18).

Clarify Your Thinking

So to say we need a revival sounds good, but it is not true because it falls short. The truth about this is indeed so much better. Revival is not our greatest need. *We need a revelation of the grace of God concerning who we are in Jesus Christ.* When we get that revelation, there is a wonderful glory that far exceeds revival. It is the source of real spiritual transformation, a process that is lifelong and permanent.

I encourage you: Pray for yourself the prayer Paul prayed for the Ephesians. Ask God to open the eyes of your heart to understand your identity and riches in Christ, and the greatness of His power available to us. You'll never be the same.

Lie #23

We Should Befriend Unbelievers in Order to Win Them

Doesn't that sound like a noble reason to befriend somebody—to win him to Christ? It's hard to criticize a believer who truly cares about leading others to faith in Jesus Christ, but we need to stop and rethink that whole idea about befriending people for that reason.

Because of who we are—loving children of a loving God—we befriend and love people simply because that's our nature. It is simply who we are. To befriend and love a person simply for the purpose of leading him to faith in Jesus Christ means that you have developed a relationship with them with a hidden motive in mind. What they think is sincerity is actually sneakiness! As well intentioned as it sounds, to befriend people just for the purpose of gaining a convert treats people as objects to be manipulated rather than as people for whom Christ died. We aren't salespeople who are looking to close the deal. We are expressions of *agapē* to the world in which we live. There's a big difference between the two.

Don't misunderstand—wanting to see people come to trust Christ is a good thing. I think that's the heart's desire of any sincere Christian. We know the joy of understanding the gospel and walking in its reality. We want to see others personally experience the reality of this life in

Christ too. Certainly, the Lord wants to see that happen. But we are to love people and befriend them. Not for a hidden agenda, but because Christ lives in us, and He simply loves people. He loves them whether they are believers or unbelievers. God doesn't love you because you believe, and He doesn't withhold love from those who don't believe.

The Truth Is So Much Better!

There's a very famous story in the New Testament, one that is as misunderstood and wrongly taught as any I know. It's often called "The Story of the Rich Young Ruler."

> As He was setting out on a journey, a man ran up to Him and knelt before Him, and asked Him, "Good Teacher, what shall I do to inherit eternal life?"
>
> And Jesus said to him, "Why do you call Me good? No one is good except God alone. You know the commandments, 'Do not murder, Do not commit adultery, Do not steal, Do not bear false witness, Do not defraud, Honor your father and mother.'"
>
> And he said to Him, "Teacher, I have kept all these things from my youth up" (Mark 10:17-20).

This story has often been discussed and debated because of Jesus telling this man, "Sell all you possess and give to the poor, and you will have treasure in heaven; and come, follow Me." People have sometimes been puzzled by that direction. Does Jesus really call all of us to sell everything we have? Is that really what He expects? If that were truly the bar we would have to get over to obtain eternal life, not many people in history would make it.

That point of view misses what this story is really all about. Already, the theme of the conversation is set. This young man called Jesus "good." He wants to know what "good" thing he can do to be sure he has eternal life. Jesus, however, has already sized him up, and replies with a major hint: "Why do you call Me good? No one is good except God alone."

If the young man were spiritually attuned, he would have seen the point right then and there. The point is that nobody is truly good apart from miraculous intervention, so he might as well give up hope of reaching heaven on the basis of goodness. This man is blinded by his own morality, though. *He thinks he is good.* He claims to have kept all the commandments from childhood, even though Jesus has just said, "No one is good except God alone." The young man totally missed it.

Since the man thought he was so good, Jesus just raised the bar to show him the truth about that matter. Jesus tells him to sell everything because this guy thought he was a great keeper of the Law, and Jesus wanted him to see he wasn't what he thought he was.

"Okay," Jesus might have said to him. "So, you love your neighbor as yourself? Well, then, it would be a small thing to give away what you possess to help your neighbor." Of course, the man turned white as a sheet. Jesus was pulling out all the stops to let the Law reveal the man's sin, which is exactly what Law does. The man was unwilling to do that, so he went away downcast.

What does this have to do with the lie that we should befriend people so that we can lead them to Christ? The answer is linked to an interesting phrase in the story. Right after the young man claims to have kept the Law, we encounter this statement: "Looking at him, *Jesus felt a love for him*" (Mark 10:21).

Now here's a question: Do you think Jesus knew from the beginning that this man was going to turn and walk away without believing? Of course He did. And yet with that full knowledge of how this man was going to respond, the Bible says Jesus looked at him and felt love for him. Jesus' love was not reserved only for those going the right direction.

Clarify Your Thinking

Don't love people with an ulterior motive in mind. Let's just love people. After all, that's who you are! The truth is, if you befriend somebody only for the purpose of bringing them to faith in Christ, people sense it. They tend to know when we have a hidden agenda that we're not telling them. So let's set that aside and love folks because Christ in us does. God is love, and when we get in touch with our authentic selves, we'll see that our desire is to love people too.

Here's the unexpected plus to this whole scenario: When you do love people the way Jesus does—unconditionally—don't be surprised if unbelievers become attracted to the Christ in you and want you to give them more information about what it means to be a follower of Christ.

Our Father loves people. He just does. So let's allow that to be good enough for us.

We Need to Pay the Price to Be Used by God

The desire to be a person who expresses the love of Christ is inherent to those who know Jesus. It's a desire that He put there, and we would all do fine if we just focused on Him and allow Him to be who He is in us and then through us as we relate to others. The problem comes when a legalistic viewpoint smothers the pure desire of our hearts and the simplicity of the gospel at work in us.

As has been noted in earlier chapters, legalism is all about what we do, as opposed to what Christ has already done. So when the wet blanket of religious legalism is thrown over the burning fire in our hearts to be used by God, the flames of inspiration are put out, and the only thing we're left with is a cold sense of obligation. We move from living out of the overflow of His life within us to a place where we think we have to make something happen.

That's where the lie is introduced to us to further intensify our wrongheaded notion about how we are to be used as an instrument in our Father's hand. Many of us have been told that God wants to use our lives, but there's a price we must pay. This kind of message often comes through impassioned preaching that is intended to stimulate you to *do something!* Pay the price! The kind of price depends on the context of your religious instruction.

For some, paying the price means being more involved in church activities. To others, it means stepping things up in your prayer life and Bible study. Some are led to think they must fast to have the breakthrough to the next level of spiritual usefulness they desire. The list could go on and on, and it will vary depending on a person's denominational culture or religious background.

Some people like this kind of challenge because they are wired for hard work anyway. It suits their personality perfectly. This teaching appeals to many because it calls upon their own sense of self-sufficiency to do something in order to warrant God taking them and using them for His glory. It's deeply rooted in the flesh (the way we try to manage our own lives independent of God). We want to contribute something.

Others, however, are discouraged by it because they have doubts about whether they can ever work long enough and successfully enough to reach a place where God could actually use them. They have an inferiority complex when it comes to their faith, and they believe they'll never qualify to be used by God.

Whichever category you fall into, it's important to rethink the premise. Does the Bible say that? Do we have to pay a "price"? If so, what "price"? What does a "price" look like? What does it mean to be "used" in this context? By looking at the Scriptures, we'll discover that it is like so many of the other lies we've discussed: It's based on a biblical truth, but somehow it has become twisted and misapplied.

The Truth Is So Much Better!

What does God ask of us? His followers came to Him one day and "said to Him, 'What shall we do, so that we may work the works of God?'" (John 6:28). The question is as clear as can be: "What do we have to do? What price must be paid for us to be used by God?"

If there were any price for us to pay, this would have been the perfect chance for Jesus to announce it. He didn't tell them anything they had to do, though. Jesus gave a clear and unambiguous answer to this question: "This is the work of God, that you *believe* in Him whom He has sent" (John 6:29).

This answer was as straightforward as it gets. In fact, the Lord's answer here is so clear that it's mind-boggling how people through the centuries could have come to any other conclusion. The only condition for doing the works of the Father is faith in Him. Period. There is no price left for us to pay because it has already been paid in full. Our role is simply to rest in and live out of His finished work!

Do you want to see the Father work through you in your daily routine? Then just trust Him and move forward in faith. It's that simple.

I love Isaiah 26:12. It says that God has "performed for us all our works." It's not up to you to pay some price to be used by God. He has already arranged the things He will do through you before you ever did one of them!

In the New Testament, Paul said it this way: "We are His workmanship, created in Christ Jesus for good works, which *God prepared in advance beforehand* so that we would walk in them" (Ephesians 2:10). To be used by Him isn't contingent on our plan and our ability to pay the price so that we qualify to be used in service. You have been created with a destiny of supernatural usefulness already lined up for you in advance.

These verses clearly say that we don't make things happen by paying a price. We simply trust our Father and walk out the plan He arranged for us long ago. To take this grace-filled approach takes the pressure off us and allows us to relax as we supernaturally express divine works in the normal routine of daily living.

Clarify Your Thinking

Our triune God has made the plan to use your life. Through the finished work of the cross, every barrier that would prevent you from realizing that plan has been removed. There's no price left to pay. The only thing to do now is to trust Him and yield ourselves completely into His guidance, wisdom, and power.

It's not about our ability to qualify for usefulness in His kingdom. It's only about our availability. The apostle Paul explained it in Romans 12:1 when he wrote, "Therefore I urge you, brethren, by the mercies of God, to present your bodies a living and holy sacrifice, acceptable to God, which is your spiritual service of worship."

It isn't about the price you pay. It is about whether you will present your availability to the Lord, just as Jesus presented His humanity to the Father every day of His time on earth.

Lie #25

We Need a Fresh Anointing

The idea of needing a fresh anointing merits mentioning in this book because it is such a widely spread teaching in some quarters of the church these days. To hear some preachers talk, a fresh anointing of the Spirit is the answer to every challenge we face in life. They think it'll cause the big breakthrough in life we've been longing for.

This teaching is problematic because it implies that we lack something we still need God to give us. Like many of the lies we're discussing in this book, this one sounds great on the surface. But ask those who say that we need a fresh anointing, "What exactly do you *mean* by that?" and you'll discover their view is inconsistent with the Bible's teaching. Most people are referring to some additional empowering by God when they talk about an "anointing." It's as though God is supposed to supersize the power of the Holy Spirit within them.

My intent isn't to criticize people's sincere desires, but I do think we need to correct misperceptions like this. Otherwise, we stray into trouble when we use terms and expressions that do not reflect biblical usage. That's exactly the case here.

What is an "anointing" about anyway? Its origins go back to the Old Testament period. In the Old Testament, an anointing was literally the act of pouring oil on a person's head. It was a symbol of God's appointment and empowerment of a person to play a special role—whether as a priest, king, or some other special service. Aaron was anointed as the first high priest when the Law of Moses began. The prophet Samuel anointed Saul and David as kings of Israel. Individual priests were anointed when they assumed their offices. Again, the meaning is the giving of authority and power to serve God in a special capacity.

The ultimate "Anointed One" is Jesus Christ. Here's something interesting: Many people assume that *Jesus* is His first name and *Christ* is His last name. But *Christ* is His title. It means "Anointed One." It comes from the Greek version of the Hebrew *Messiah*, which means the same thing.

That's why Jesus was making a messianic claim when He visited the synagogue in His hometown and selected Isaiah 61:1-2 to read:

> "The Spirit of the Lord is upon Me, because *He anointed Me* to preach the gospel to the poor. He has sent Me to proclaim release to the captives, and recovery of sight to the blind, to set free those who are oppressed, to proclaim the favorable year of the Lord"...And He began to say to them, "Today this Scripture has been fulfilled in your hearing" (Luke 4:18-21).

The implications of this claim didn't escape the people who were listening. In fact, as Jesus continued, they were angered by what He said and rose up to try to kill Him.

Jesus' anointing for His role as Messiah came at His baptism by John when the Holy Spirit descended upon Him and the Father said, "This is My beloved Son." That's when His humanity was declared ready to embark on public ministry.

What about us? Can we be "anointed" too? The answer is a definite "yes," but how and when it happens might surprise you.

The Truth Is So Much Better!

The New Testament rarely speaks of a spiritual anointing, but what it does say is clear. Because of the presence of Christ within you, *you already have been anointed.* Look at what Paul wrote: "Now He who establishes us with you in Christ and *anointed us* is God, who also sealed us and gave us the Spirit in our hearts as a pledge" (2 Corinthians 1:21-22).

John also wrote about this anointing. In describing his confidence in his readers' ability to discern truth from error, he wrote, "But you *have* an anointing from the Holy One, and you all know" (1 John 2:20). Note that John didn't say these believers needed it. He said they had it.

Keep in mind that John isn't talking here about some special category of believers, but of *all* believers. He continues, "These things I have written to you concerning those who are trying to deceive you. As for you, the *anointing which you have received from Him abides in you,* and you have no need for anyone to teach you; but as *His anointing teaches you* about all things, and is true and is not a lie, and just as it has taught you, you abide in Him" (1 John 2:26-27).

So how do we put this together? First, Jesus Christ Himself is the anointing of God. In the temple, He basically said, "Do you want to see the Anointing of Almighty God? You're looking at Him!" The Holy Spirit of Christ who lives in us is divine empowerment. That's what the anointing is all about. His life is inside you at this very moment, and you have the anointing for that reason. The anointing is a person named Jesus, and He never leaves you.

Clarify Your Thinking

Don't misunderstand me. I am not criticizing people's good intentions or their desire for themselves or others to be used by God in great ways. It's an admirable desire to be mightily used by God. That seems to be the main thing people mean by *anointing* today. I've often had people pray for me before I speak, and they say, "Lord, anoint him in a special way." I know what they mean (and so does God, of course), and I appreciate the prayer.

I don't want to nitpick words, but unbiblical language can potentially promote misunderstanding about the subject being discussed. Many believers, for instance, have erroneously thought that others—especially gifted leaders—are "anointed," having something from God that the rest of believers don't. They may think that "anointing" is for special believers who are at a different spiritual level than they are themselves. Some people even think it's not for "ordinary Christians." The Bible teaches exactly the opposite.

The anointing is a person named Jesus, and He lives in you. You are anointed, and that's a fact. Now you only need to act like it. When we know we have the anointing of the resident Christ living in us and then act as though it's true, that reality will empower us to live triumphantly and victoriously. God will live through us, and people will be amazed.

Repentance Brings God's Goodness into Our Lives

Many people in the modern church world badly abuse the topic of repentance. The subject is vulnerable to a legalistic perspective because legalism suggests that we can get God to respond to us by what we do. But the truth of grace is this: The Father acts in love toward us first, and then we respond to Him.

The idea that repentance brings God's blessings to our lives is a prevalent, legalistic teaching in the church. This teaching is as old covenant as you can possibly get. Because of the finished work of Jesus Christ at the cross, the truth now under the new covenant is exactly the opposite. God's goodness causes us to repent. We don't repent to cause God to act in goodness toward us. We repent because He *has* acted in goodness toward us.

Sometimes critics of the grace walk message will say, "Where's repentance in your message?" Many people who ask that question are thinking about the old-fashioned, revivalist-type fire-and-brimstone preaching. "You'd better repent of your sins—things such as lying, stealing, adultery, gambling, drinking, smoking, and dancing—and *then* God will respond favorably toward you!" If you grew up in that environment, you know the routine.

There are a lot of things wrong with this whole approach, but let's first consider what repentance really means. What is repentance? Many people confuse it with remorse, which is to feel badly about something you've done. They think, "You haven't really repented unless you are groveling and wallowing in your guilt and shame. That's how you will allow God to release good into your life."

Although that view is common, it's not what the Bible means by repentance. The New Testament was written in Greek, and the word *repentance* is the Greek word *metanoia*. It comes from two words. The first (*meta*) means "after," and the second (*noieō*) means "to think as the result of observing." So the word *repent* in the New Testament is a compound word that means "to think differently after taking a closer look at a matter." Simply put, it means to change your mind. It's an about-face in the way you think. It's an afterthought, and it's different from what we thought before we looked closer. So repentance, then, isn't about groveling before God and being racked with guilt and shame. It's about changing our minds.

The Truth Is So Much Better!

The apostle Paul clearly showed the relationship between repentance and God's goodness when he wrote to the church at Rome. He asked them, "Do you think lightly of the riches of His kindness and tolerance and patience, not knowing that the kindness of God leads you to repentance?" (Romans 2:4). So which comes first—God's goodness or repentance? The answer is made clear in Paul's words.

We don't cause God to act favorably toward us by what we do. That is a legalistic perspective regardless of the subject we're discussing, and repentance is included. Paul raised the point that the kindness, tolerance, and patience of our Father motivates us to repent. That's the grace template. He expresses His loving goodness to us, and we respond in faith and obedience to Him.

Clarify Your Thinking

The fountainhead of God's goodness is in the message of His amazing love and grace. When we understand the unconditional love of our

Father and the infinite grace He has toward us, that understanding motivates us to change our minds about Him and ourselves. Our repentant minds then become the catalyst for a change in our behavior.

The reason so many people in the modern church are struggling with the concept of repentance is because they think it all hinges on their ability to rehabilitate their behavior. These same people constantly feel like their inability to truly repent (as they understand it) is what keeps them from experiencing God's goodness in full measure. But we don't have the power in and of ourselves to change the way we live.

We need to change the way we understand the love the Father has for us. *That* is the repentance people need in their minds. When we come to understand His love for us, we will discover that we *want* to ensure that our actions remain consistent with the love we have for Him.

Paul wrote that "the love of Christ compels us" (2 Corinthians 5:14 NIV). Note that it does not say our love for Him does this. His love for us becomes our motivator. That fact is largely unknown by many people today. They mistakenly think that the key to motivation toward godly living is to love Him, but Paul said that just the opposite is the case. *His* love for *us* compels us to live righteously.

Repentance isn't turning over a new leaf in your lifestyle. It's having your mind turn in the opposite direction. A change in behavior will come, but it is the secondary effect of repentance, not the essence of it.

Don't believe the lie that you must repent in order to experience God's goodness. Your Father's loving goodness toward you is unconditional and independent of anything you do or don't do. When you understand and believe that, you'll be amazed by how your behavior will line up with your repentant mind.

Lie #27

Grace and Truth Need to Be Kept in Balance

The assertion that grace and truth need to be kept in balance is one of the predictable objections to the undiluted message of God's grace. This lie is particularly dangerous because the concept of balance in life is so prevalent and in many cases correct. For example, finding balance between work and leisure is a good thing. Finding a balance between saving money and hoarding is important. The list could go on, but the idea of balance doesn't apply in every way imaginable. For instance, finding a balance between fidelity and infidelity in marriage makes no sense. Sometimes the attempt to apply the concept of balance simply doesn't fit. That's the case when it comes to truth and grace.

Nobody who takes the Bible seriously can deny its teaching about grace. At the same time, there are those who struggle with the pure, undiluted grace of God, so they take the concept of balance and try to apply it here. They can't very well *deny* the grace of God—it's too evident in Scripture. But they'll try to tone it down with this argument: "Well, yes," they say. "Grace is a wonderful truth. But you have to keep grace and truth in balance with each other so you don't go to an extreme." Since few people want to be "extreme," that seems to make reasonable sense.

This approach is problematic because it draws a line down the middle and puts grace on one side and truth on the other, as if the two are in opposition to each another. It's as if they're saying that grace is not truth and truth is not grace. That's not what the Bible says. Grace and truth do not stand in contrast to each other. The Bible puts grace and truth on the same side of the line. Grace is truth, and the truth is grace. To separate them as I've described is a legalistic way to interpret God's grace.

The Truth Is So Much Better!

Does the Bible teach a balance between grace and truth as though the two are separate realities? It does not. To the contrary, Scripture inseparably joins the two together in the person of Jesus Christ. The Bible says, "The Law was given through Moses; grace and truth were realized through Jesus Christ" (John 1:17).

John says here that grace and truth came to fullness (to fruition) in the person of Jesus Christ. He wasn't *part* grace and *part* truth. He was 100 percent grace and 100 percent truth! You can find the qualities of both in Christ. They're in perfect harmony and unity. All by itself, John 1:17 proves that grace and truth are not opposed to one another.

If you're going to draw a line, draw it between grace and legalism—not between grace and truth. The Bible plainly puts grace and truth on the same side of the line, in Jesus. So anytime you hear people say, "Well, this message of grace is good, but you have to balance that with truth," you can recognize what they are doing. Whether they are sincerely mistaken or committed legalists, you can know that it's a lie, because grace and truth are not on two different sides of the dividing line. They're on the *same* side of the line. Legalism is on the other side of the line. Grace and truth are synonymous because they are expressed (or personified) in the person of Jesus Christ, who is "full of grace and truth."

Why do we struggle so much with this? Admittedly, human beings often aren't in balance. We do tend to lean toward different extremes.

But let's not confuse this matter of grace and truth. Grace and truth are in perfect harmony. There's nothing to balance between them. They're perfectly complementary.

Clarify Your Thinking

The lie that we need to find a balance between grace and truth might sound good to those who don't know better, but I can't overstate the devastating effect of attempting to divide the two. Grace and truth are conjoined twins. You cannot separate them without killing both.

To suggest that we should find balance within the topic of grace is an insidious lie. Any attempt to do that is to compromise grace. Grace is Jesus, and He doesn't need to be balanced with anything. Balance Him with truth? Reject that nonsense. He *is* truth!

Whether they know it or not, people who say that we need to maintain a balance in the teaching of grace are suggesting that it needs to be watered down so that it's not so offensive to the legalist. Remember, the legalist feels like there must be something that we have to contribute to this life we have received in Christ. But as we've discussed, you can't add anything. You already have Jesus, and He is grace *and* truth—the whole truth and nothing but the truth.

Lie #28

God Only Speaks Today Through the Bible

If you suggest that our God speaks to us in any way outside the Bible, you'll walk on thin ice with many people. Make no mistake about the fact that your Father will never speak to you in a way that contradicts what the Bible says. But the teaching that He can only speak to you when you read the Bible is a lie, and it will prevent you from hearing Him at many other times. Our God speaks in many ways, and if we have the ears to hear Him speak in those ways, we will find unlimited opportunities to hear His voice.

He can speak to us through nature. Have you never heard Him declare His greatness as you stared into the starry night sky? He speaks through music. Remember the times your heart has been stirred as you've listened to somebody sing a particular song that you knew was speaking directly to you? He certainly can speak to us through other people. Haven't you ever talked to a friend in a time of need and found that they had said something to you that helped? Maybe they gave you advice or encouraged you in some way, and you believed you heard the voice of the Lord in it. God speaks through culture, art, circumstances, and countless other ways.

Some people may think I'm diminishing the value of the Bible, but I'm not. I'm magnifying the ability of our Father to speak to us. If you limit Him by your perspective, you'll do yourself a great disservice.

The Truth Is So Much Better!

The psalmist wrote that the Bible itself affirms the fact that God speaks to the human race in other ways:

> The heavens are telling of the glory of God; and their expanse is declaring the work of His hands. Day to day pours forth speech, and night to night reveals knowledge. There is no speech, nor are there words; their voice is not heard. Their line has gone out through all the earth, and their utterances to the end of the world (Psalm 19:1-4).

The Scripture says that the heavens declare the glory of God. As this Psalm says, there is no audible voice, but "their utterances" go out "to the end of the world." The voice of the Creator comes through the heavens. The Lord is the one speaking, declaring His glory to us through nature. In Romans 1:18-21, Paul says that the whole world can see God through the things He has created. The evidence is undeniable.

However, there is much more. Hebrews 1:1-2 says, "God, after He spoke long ago to the fathers in the prophets in many portions and in many ways, in these last days has spoken to us in His Son, whom He appointed heir of all things, through whom also He made the world."

The Father's ultimate expression to us is through His Son, Jesus Christ. Our God hasn't stopped speaking. He is still speaking to us because Christ *is* the Word of God and He lives and is still active. Remember how John described Jesus in the beginning of his Gospel?

> In the beginning was the Word, and the Word was with God, and *the Word was God.* He was in the beginning with God. All things came into being through Him, and apart from Him nothing came into being that has come into being...

And *the Word became flesh,* and dwelt among us, and we saw His glory, glory as of the only begotten from the Father, full of grace and truth (John 1:1-3,14).

Who is Jesus Christ? He is the living Word of God who has taken on a human nature and body, the Word of God now made visible and audible. And this same Jesus, now risen and glorified, lives in you and me!

Clarify Your Thinking

If you believe the lie that God speaks only through the Bible, then the enemy only needs to keep you from reading the Bible to keep you from hearing your divine lover. Don't fall for the lie. God does speak through the Bible, but if you restrict yourself to that alone, you'll miss many opportunities to hear His loving voice throughout your day.

It's a Sin to Be Depressed

H ere's one that has caused people who are already hurting terribly to be even more injured. Sincere but mistaken people hold many of the lies I'm challenging, but some of the lies are more damaging than others. The resistance I received on the Internet surprised me when I first posted that it's not a sin to be depressed. Apparently, many people in some parts of the church world think it is our birthright as Christians to never feel emotionally low. I couldn't disagree more, and neither could the Bible.

Let's clarify the meaning of the word *depression* first. That way, we'll be sure we're thinking of the same thing in this chapter. What do we mean by saying that a person is *depressed?* The word can have different meaning to different people. Sometimes, we simply mean that we feel emotionally down. We have been disappointed by circumstances or hurt by someone. To some people, the word means that we are simply feeling emotionally depleted after a time of great stress. Sometimes people are talking about the blues. Some ups and downs are normal aspects of human life, and we come around after a time of recreation, rest, or sleep.

Some people might say they are depressed because of serious

circumstances in their lives. If you've lost a loved one, mate, child, or parent through death—if you've suffered great loss—it would be normal to feel emotional pain for more than a fleeting moment. Normal grief is a normal reaction to that kind of thing, and it can bring temporary depression. Most of us can say that we would understand such a reaction. We can have peace at the deepest level of our being but still feel emotionally troubled by life's circumstances.

Sometimes a deeper, darker emotion we call "depression" stems from choices to indulge anger and wallow in self-pity. This kind of depression can be dark indeed, and it can progress to even more serious forms.

Finally, there can be physiological reasons for depression. It could be because of a hormonal imbalance, and it could be because of some sort of imbalance in the chemicals in the brain. It can stem from an unknown physical cause. This genuine clinical form of depression is a medical condition, and it needs to be addressed by trained medical and therapeutic professionals. It is dangerous because it could even lead to life-threatening problems. Even people who have lived decades happily and responsibly have run into this monster, and they see themselves collapse and become nonfunctional. If you have this type of depression, your brain—which, remember, is an organ—simply cannot function properly. The chemicals necessary for a functioning brain are lacking.

Then along come some "spiritual" Christians who proclaim that depression is a sin, adding to the pain of those who are in the middle of one of these legitimate types of depression. Those suffering believers then have guilt added to the pain they already feel, and they begin thinking that God must be angry at them too because of their inability to overcome their "sin."

Be assured that it is a wrong approach to try to connect the dots between emotional feelings and the level of spiritual victory that we have in life. The truth is, you can be very low emotionally and still be strong spiritually. I used to think that it was a sin to be depressed emotionally, but that was until I really began to get into the Bible and study the lives of believers of the past centuries. I found there were many great saints of God who were depressed. And the Bible in no way indicates that it was a sin. Remember, depression is heaviness in the soul—the mind, will, and emotions.

Anxiety in our emotions is a normal part of the human experience. Sometimes people say to me, "Is it right or wrong for me to be depressed about this or that?" I've answered, "What if we don't approach the subject in terms of 'right and wrong'? Let's simply look at it this way: It's human and natural that you would feel the way you do."

The Truth Is So Much Better!

Job did not hide his emotions through his great trials. In fact, he was quite candid:

> Even today my complaint is rebellion; His hand [God's hand] is heavy despite my groaning. Oh that I knew where I might find Him, that I might come to His seat! I would present my case before Him and fill my mouth with arguments. I would learn the words which He would answer, and perceive what He would say to me. Would He contend with me by the greatness of His power? No, surely He would pay attention to me. There the upright would reason with Him; and I would be delivered forever from my Judge. Behold, I go forward but He is not there, and backward, but I cannot perceive Him; When He acts on the left, I cannot behold Him; He turns on the right, I cannot see Him (Job 23:2-9).

Again and again in the book of Job, he expressed his negative emotions. He even said, "I wish I'd never been born," and he wasn't sure that life made any sense. These nine verses in Job 23 are a very articulate and strong declaration of his emotional depression.

But listen to what he says in the next verse: "But He knows the way that I take; when He has tried me, I shall come forth as gold" (Job 23:10). There is Job's declaration of faith.

The Bible does not condemn us for feeling negative emotions like anger, fear, anxiety, or depression. God recognizes that life's circumstances are often too much for us to carry.

Some may say that things changed in the New Testament, but apparently the apostle Paul didn't agree with that. He described a time when he was emotionally exhausted to the Corinthians:

> We do not want you to be unaware, brethren, of our affliction which came to us in Asia, that we were burdened excessively, beyond our strength, so that we despaired even of life; indeed, we had the sentence of death within ourselves so that we would not trust in ourselves, but in God who raises the dead (2 Corinthians 1:8-10).

There's simply no way to put a positive spin on what Paul wrote here. It would take great mental gymnastics to think he was describing anything other than the emotional bankruptcy he had felt while he was ministering in Asia.

Clarify Your Thinking

Don't be judgmental of other people who are emotionally depressed. It may be only by the grace of God that you aren't in the same place yourself! And if you do go through it, don't judge yourself for it.

Calling emotional depression a sin is a lie. It is a part of the human experience. We do need to choose carefully what we do with the emotional reactions that we have in life, but that's another teaching for another time. This is the point I want you to recognize: Sometimes emotional depression is the normal and natural reaction to things that are going on. If you believe otherwise, you will remain in bondage to feelings of guilt and shame. You might also unintentionally bring condemnation to other hurting people. Believe that Christ is your peace and your joy, and He will guide you step by step. And He will embrace you...even in the middle of your depression.

Lie #30

You Should Make Jesus Lord of Your Life

Perhaps no lie mentioned in this book has caused more controversy than this one. The debate over "Lordship salvation," as it's called, has been going on for years among some theologians. Some people argue that a person isn't a Christian unless he has made Jesus Christ Lord of his life. Others contend that it is possible to know Him as Savior and learn about Lordship later. Whichever side of that debate you may find yourself on, one commonly hears from both sides that we are to make Jesus Lord of our lives.

I've irritated more than a few people in the past by suggesting that this whole debate about "Lordship salvation" is silly. Jesus is not just Savior. He's not just Lord either. He is our very *life*.

If we believe that we must make Jesus Lord of our lives, that view presents a problem in our attitude about ourselves. *We* must make Jesus Lord? Do you see the underlying pride in that perspective? We must *make* Jesus be something? Who do we think that we are that *we* can *make* Jesus be anything?'

The straight truth of the Bible is this: Jesus Christ *is* Lord. He is King of kings and Lord of lords. That is an objective and eternal reality. We don't make Him that. He is the eternal God, and He is omnipotent, omniscient, and omnipresent—He is Lord. He is Lord whether we recognize it or not. So the teaching that we must make Jesus Lord of our lives practically deifies mankind. It's not just legalistic. It's arrogant beyond description. Jesus *is* Lord.

Some people may argue, "But that's not what I mean!" To which I would respond, "Then *say* what you mean!" Again, we don't make Jesus become anything. He is who He is, and we have nothing to contribute to that.

The Truth Is So Much Better!

The Son of God became a man and came on a mission from the Father, to "give His life a ransom for many" (Matthew 20:28). We will be grateful throughout eternity for His sacrifice, which has brought eternal life to us. As we interpret the power of His death and resurrection, we should not miss what the Father has said about the result. After describing Jesus' willing obedience to go to the cross, Scripture points out that Jesus already is Lord:

> God highly honored Him and bestowed on Him the name which is above every name, so that *at the name of Jesus every knee will bow,* of those who are in heaven and on earth and under the earth, and that *every tongue will confess that Jesus Christ is Lord,* to the glory of God the Father" (Philippians 2:9-11).

This great passage tells us that every creature will one day acknowledge the Lordship of Christ. *Every* knee, *every* tongue. No exceptions. *God* has made Jesus Lord, not man. Nothing can change that fact— not man's choice, vote, or rejection.

The risen, glorified, and ascended Jesus has been made Lord of all creation. Paul wants to describe a supreme example of God's power, focusing on Jesus' ascension in his letter to the Ephesians:

> These are in accordance with the working of the strength of His might which He brought about in Christ, when He raised Him from the dead and seated Him at His right hand

in the heavenly places, *far above all rule and authority and power and dominion, and every name that is named,* not only in this age but also in the one to come. And *He put all things in subjection under His feet* (Ephesians 1:19-22).

Jesus *has* all authority and power. He is who He is, totally apart from human response. This is the only Jesus who is. That means to trust Him as Savior means to trust *this* Jesus as Savior. There is no other. The Lordship salvation debate is silly, but it's more than that. It confuses passages on discipleship—which can be difficult and full of challenging choices—with the Bible's offer of a free salvation.

So if we cannot "make" Him Lord, what is our response to be? Paul, the one who wrote the most about the Lordship of Jesus Christ, said, "Therefore I urge you, brethren, by the mercies of God, to present your bodies a living and holy sacrifice, acceptable to God, which is your spiritual service of worship" (Romans 12:1).

As children of a God who wants us to love Him and serve Him, we can offer ourselves to Him. We can live by depending totally on Him. That's how the Lord lives His life through us. Then we can apply our faith in His Lordship by trusting Him as we experience pressure.

Regarding the times we deal with difficult people, Peter tells us, "But *sanctify Christ as Lord in your hearts,* always being ready to make a defense to everyone who asks you to give an account for the hope that is in you, yet with gentleness and reverence" (1 Peter 3:15).

What does Peter mean by "sanctify Christ as Lord in your hearts"? When people are opposing you (maybe they're making life difficult for you), it's easy to begin feeling intimidated and tongue-tied. But don't focus on them. Keep your inner eyes on Jesus Christ and entrust yourself to Him, knowing that He *is* Lord over the situation you face. He will guide you, and when opportunity presents itself, you can share the reasons for your faith in the proper spirit.

We don't have to make Him Lord. We simply *remember* and *rest* in His Lordship. We will find that single act to be sufficient.

Clarify Your Thinking

The whole idea that we must make Jesus Lord of our lives points back to *us*—what *we* need to do and what *we* think we can do. It will keep you in bondage because it will cause you to always be looking at yourself. You'll be evaluating yourself to see whether or not you measure up, and you'll always conclude that you don't.

No, it's not up to us to do that. We couldn't do it if we wanted to. He is Lord. Period.

We Need
More Faith

You may hear Christians make this statement just about any day of the week. "I need more faith." "You need more faith." "If you had more faith, you could be healed." "If we had more faith, God would do miracles." "If we had more faith, we would have this or see that…" The assumption that we don't have enough faith is almost universal in the modern church world. We shouldn't be surprised by that. Even Jesus' closest followers thought this way. "The apostles said to the Lord, 'Increase our faith'" (Luke 17:5)!

The idea is that faith comes in incremental degrees. If that's our viewpoint, we'll naturally believe that we need more. But it's not true. Faith is not given to you by degrees. Faith is given to you in the person of Jesus Christ. In fact, the Bible teaches that Christ *is* our faith.

Everyone talks about faith, but there seems to be much misunderstanding about what having it actually means. Many people have associated faith with that warm, tingly feeling they get at times when they feel spiritually moved. Others think of it as the degree of confidence (or lack of fear) they feel. *But faith is not a feeling.* A person expressing faith could feel confident or spiritually moved, but it's important to recognize that faith isn't grounded in feelings.

Biblical faith is always *objective*. It's more than a subjective feeling. It's an actual reality, and it has a concrete source. We've often been taught that the strength of faith is in the *object* of one's faith. That statement is completely true. For example, would faith in a stone idol do you any good? How about faith in a human religious leader? Could that faith help you? Of course not. It wouldn't matter how much faith you have if it is placed in an unworthy or unreliable object.

Compare faith to swallowing for a moment. Somebody could say, "Swallowing makes you live." That might sound all right at first, but consider this: Yes, you can swallow good food, and that will enable you to live. But you can also swallow poison and die. It isn't swallowing that makes you live. It's what you swallow—the object—that determines the result.

Faith is the same. A mountain-sized faith in an unworthy object will do you no good. It isn't *how much* faith you have. Think of the issue this way: *In whom* have you put that faith?

Also, the *object* of our faith is not the only thing that is important. We also have to realize the equal importance of the *source* of our faith. Faith isn't something that we work up by thinking positive thoughts and speaking positive words. Faith is personified in Jesus Christ. He doesn't just give us faith, but He *is* our faith! We live by His life and thus live by divine faith.

The Truth Is So Much Better!

By what power could we produce faith apart from the loving work of our Father within us? Even the most foundational aspect of following Jesus Christ—trusting in His finished work to provide salvation—is the result of expressing faith in Him that actually *came* from Him. Paul wrote, "By grace you have been saved through faith; and *that* not of yourselves, it is a gift of God; not as a result of works, so that no one may boast" (Ephesians 2:8-9). Grace is the cause for our salvation, and faith is the conduit through which we experience it, but the Bible says that when it comes to faith, *that* doesn't come from us. It's a gift of God. He gives us the faith we possess as a gift.

Faith isn't something we achieve by getting our minds right. It's something we receive through Jesus, and we then live by His faith, not one that we have to try to produce. The apostle Paul talked about faith in another place in Scripture that greatly comes to bear on the point I'm making here. Galatians 2:20 is often rendered as saying, "I have been crucified with Christ; and it is no longer I who live, but Christ lives in me; and the life which I now live in the flesh I live by faith in the Son of God, who loved me and gave Himself up for me."

Like the one above, most translations say that we live by faith *in* the Son of God, but the original language of the New Testament (Greek) points to a different emphasis. While it's certainly not wrong to say that we live by faith in Jesus Christ, think about how this literal translation renders the same verse: "With Christ I have been crucified, and live no more do I, and Christ doth live in me; and that which I now live in the flesh—in the faith I live of the Son of God, who did love me and did give himself for me" (YOUNG'S).

Notice the distinction here. While it's true that we live by faith in the Son of God, the complete picture is even better than that. We live by the faith *of* the Son of God!

Speaking of how Jesus set us free from the Law by His coming, the apostle Paul said this in Galatians 3:23: "Before *faith* came, we were kept in custody under the law, being shut up to the faith which was later to be revealed." If we look at the context of this passage, we can see that Paul clearly isn't just talking about belief. He is talking about Christ, who *is* our faith.

Clarify Your Thinking

The idea that we need to have more faith is a lie, and it will cause you to constantly evaluate yourself, wondering if you have enough of it. Every time you give yourself such a legalistic test, you'll conclude that you come up short. That's always the result of a legalistic approach.

The truth is that you have enough faith because you have Jesus Christ. Don't focus on *your* faith. Focus on Him and depend on His faith to sustain you. His strength is perfected in our weakness. You don't need more faith. We all simply need to more fully know all we possess in Jesus Christ. So when you feel like your faith is weak, defer to Him because His faith will never let you down.

Lie #32

Your Sins Can Disqualify You from Being Used by God

We have looked at many truths about the true identity we have because of Christ. We have seen that we have been forgiven, adopted, justified, reconciled, and sanctified. But as new creatures in Christ, we still have the capacity to sin. We all are capable of being tempted and weakened to where we can commit any sin. That's why it is important to learn how to depend on the indwelling Christ as our source for living.

The people who say they never sin are deceiving themselves, or they are blatantly telling a lie. Nobody in this world lives a sinless and perfect life. The good news is that no sin you or I can ever commit is able to undo the work of Christ! We may sin in awful ways, but we remain forgiven, justified, reconciled, adopted children. The Lord is faithful even if we are unfaithful.

It is important to hold on to the truths the Scriptures teach us, or in times of personal failure we will be ripe for a slide into total despair. Sadly, judgmental Christians and erroneous teaching often drive those who have failed to deeper despair rather than encouraging them toward hope and restoration. The lie we are considering now fits in this category.

Sometimes people contend that if you sin in a really serious way (in their judgment), you will be disqualified from being used by God. This lie infects the minds of the fallen and causes them to think that somehow they've jumped the track and that God can never take their lives and use them for His glory. When I was a legalistic pastor, I used to teach that you could commit sins so serious and so wrong that God would "set you on the shelf" and no longer be able to use your life.

This teaching is totally untrue, and it stands in harsh contrast to the grace of God. It's true that "where sin abounds, grace much more abounds." Our God's loving grace is bigger than the greatest sin. The message of grace is that He can redeem your weaknesses and even turn your sinful behavior around and use you for His glory. God can overcome the circumstances of your life, no matter what you might have done. He can restore your life, and He can turn things around and use your life in ways greater than you can imagine.

I used to say about some sins, "Well, you can't unscramble eggs." That saying is true if it means the past can't be changed, but God actually does something much better than that. He is the God of new beginnings and resurrections. He is the God who makes things new. He is the God of the now! His name is "I Am," not "I Was."

We serve a God who takes eggs that have been scrambled and—rather than unscrambling them—creates from them a totally new thing you would never think of in a million years. His recipes for life are divine.

The Truth Is So Much Better!

People usually think of biblical characters in exalted terms, as if they were part of a different class of human beings than we are. "Of course they were righteous and holy. They're in the Bible!" If that's your view, then maybe you need to look a little more carefully. Hebrews 11 is known as the great "faith chapter" of the New Testament. It lists many heroes of the faith and tells a little about them. However, it doesn't tell everything. Take a close look at their life stories as they are recorded in the Old Testament, and you'll learn that these people were far from perfect in the way they acted at times.

Consider a few of the people mentioned in that chapter. Noah was a faithful man who built the ark. But no sooner had he come off the ark, you see him falling down drunk. Abraham, Israel's greatest patriarch, gave into fear and lied in an attempt to pass off his wife as his sister, involving her in the deceptive scheme—and not once, but twice! The great Lawgiver of the old covenant, Moses, killed a man. Samson, the great hero and judge, and David, the king who was the "man after God's own heart," are on this list—even though they both committed immoralities and adulteries that are remembered to this day. David compounded his sin of adultery by conspiring to bring about the death of Bathsheba's husband as a cover-up. In Hebrews 11:31, the Bible mentions Rahab the harlot. Most people would consider prostitution to be a great sin, and yet she was used by the Lord to protect His people of Israel. She later married into the nation of Israel, and she became an ancestor of King David, the ancestor of Jesus. Think about that for a moment. Rahab the harlot is an ancestor of *Jesus Christ*, the Lord of heaven and earth.

All the people mentioned in the Bible had flaws, and some of their sins are described in gory detail in Scripture. However, as is true for us today, God's grace was greater than their foolish choices. This is how Hebrews 11 sums up the lives of those Old Testament believers: "All these…gained approval through their faith" (Hebrews 11:39).

The New Testament teaches the same about the people whose lives it describes. If I were to ask you to name the greatest follower of Jesus that ever lived, whose name would you say? I suspect most people would say the apostle Paul. Listen to what he said about himself: "You have heard of my former manner of life in Judaism, how I used to persecute the church of God beyond measure and tried to destroy it" (Galatians 1:13). In another place, he said, "I persecuted this Way [Christians] to the death, binding and putting both men and women into prisons" (Acts 22:4).

The apostle Paul had been a violent persecutor of believers and even murdered some of them, and yet the Lord used him to establish churches throughout the Mediterranean world and write two thirds of the New Testament.

Someone might argue, "But unlike Paul, my sins were committed *after* I became a Christian." All right, then, what about Simon Peter? Peter, who had lived and walked and served with Jesus for most of three years, turned away from Him. Peter denied Jesus after His arrest, and he ran out in shame and guilt. He was nowhere to be found at the crucifixion. I'm sure he wondered if the Lord would ever be able to use him again. But when Jesus was raised from the dead, the angel at the tomb said, "Go, tell His disciples *and Peter*" (Mark 16:7). He specifically mentioned him by name. I think the reason Peter was mentioned by name is because the Lord wanted to let him know that he was still loved and forgiven. God's grace was bigger than Peter's colossal blunder.

We are told later that the Lord's mercy for Peter was so great that He appeared to him one-on-one: "And they got up that very hour and returned to Jerusalem, and found gathered together the eleven and those who were with them, saying, 'The Lord has really risen and *has appeared to Simon*' (Luke 24:33-34).

What a picture of the grace of God! He didn't write off Peter or "put him on the shelf." He restored him and put him into His service again, even into the position of key leadership among the apostles.

Clarify Your Thinking

Look back over your past and think about the very worst thing you've ever done. Now take that thing in your mind and lay it down at the foot of the cross. Then walk away and leave it there. The idea that you can commit sins that will disqualify you from being used by God is so untrue.

Don't believe that you've done something so terrible that God can't use your life. There's nothing you've ever done and nothing you could ever do that would keep God from working both in and through your life. The idea that you can commit sins that can disqualify you from being used by God is a lie, and it will keep you in bondage. You can be made ineffective by giving in to the despair and losing hope, but that isn't the work of God. God wants you to hope in Christ and His promises, and He wants you to get up and allow Him to restore you and lead you to where you can serve Him.

Lie #33

You Need to Starve the Old Nature and Feed the New

This lie reminds me of the famous line from the comic-strip character Pogo: "We have met the enemy and he is us." It was a clever comic, but in expressing theology this phrase is a totally wrong viewpoint. Sadly, many Christians have embraced this outlook about themselves and believe there is an evil side within them—an evil nature—that fights against the new nature given to us by Christ.

The big problem with this lie is that it implies a Christian still has two natures. But nothing could be further from the truth. The Bible teaches that, at the cross, our old nature was crucified along with Christ. It's not there—because it was put to death. Although I'm not suggesting we now live sinless, perfect lives, it's no longer our *nature* to sin.

It's true we experience a conflict between the inclinations to give in to temptation and to resist it. But this conflict has nothing to do with having an old nature within us that hungers to sin. In fact, if you really had both an old and a new nature within you, then you would be set up for failure. As Jesus said about Satan—and the principle applies here—"If a house is divided against itself, that house cannot stand." Your loving God wouldn't put you in such a hopeless state.

The Truth Is So Much Better!

The Bible teaches that the nature that came to us in Adam has been crucified and permanently put to death. Romans 6:6 tells us that "our old man was crucified with Him, that the body of sin might be done away with, that we should no longer be slaves of sin" (NKJV).

"Old man" is the term Paul uses to describe the nature Adam passed down to his descendants (often called the Adamic nature). But you as a believer aren't in Adam. You are in Christ. The Bible plainly teaches that the old man, who was in Adam, was crucified. Crucifixion doesn't cause just a weakening. It causes *death*. The Bible says that our body of sin, which once empowered the sinful lifestyle, has been destroyed. Think of the word "body" in Romans 6:6 in the way you would think of a "body of evidence" in a court case. The word indicates the *source* of something. In this case, the source that gave power to sin in your life has been destroyed. That source was the old nature, and it has been crucified and buried with Christ. It will never come back to life again!

For many years I believed I possessed two natures that were in conflict, and I thought the solution to the problem was to "feed" the new nature and "starve" the old one. I believed I could do that by refusing to indulge what I thought was my old nature and by feeding the "new man" the things he enjoyed, such as Bible study, prayer, and participation in religious activities with other believers.

If you imagine you have two natures competing for preeminence within you, you have fallen victim to this lie. You don't have two natures. Your old man was crucified with Christ. Because we were crucified with Jesus (see Galatians 2:20 below), we don't have that nature. The Bible clearly teaches that the old you died:

- "You have died and your life is hidden with Christ in God" (Colossians 3:3).

- "Do you not know that as all of us who have been baptized into Christ Jesus, have been baptized into His death?" (Romans 6:3).

If we don't believe that our old, Adamic nature died, we face the difficult question of answering what *did* die—because the fact of the matter is, something died.

I used to argue with the idea that the old man died. But if it wasn't the old man that died, as Paul plainly said in Romans 6:6, then what did die? The truth is, it was that old, Adamic nature that died with Jesus Christ. Paul said in Galatians 2:20, "I have been crucified with Christ; and it is no longer I who live."

Clarify Your Thinking

The lie is that the old man is still there competing for preeminence in your life. The truth is that the old man was put to death with Jesus Christ on the cross, and the battles you and I have now are not with our old man. Instead, the battle is with the power of indwelling sin, as Paul describes in Romans 7. Make no mistake about it, indwelling sin and the old man (the old nature) are two totally different things. We still have a propensity to sin because we have the same physical bodies we have always had, and for that reason the power of sin affects us. (See Romans 7:16-25.) But it is not our nature to sin anymore.

If you believe, at the core of your being, that you possess an evil nature that seeks to rise up and take control of you, that lie will empower the enemy to deceive you into thinking you are helpless to consistently live a righteous lifestyle. Over the long haul, none of us will act in a way that contradicts what we believe about ourselves. So if you believe you are wicked in the deep, hidden places of your life, that deception will become a catalyst for sinful behavior. However, understanding the truth that you are not wicked but have, in fact, received the very nature of Jesus Christ will enable you to rise up and live like the godly person you are!

This chapter isn't intended simply to make you feel good about yourself by giving you a positive self-image. My goal here is to help you see yourself as God sees you! You need a *godly* self-image. The apostle Peter said that believers have become "partakers of the divine nature" (see 2 Peter 1:3-4). You aren't some kind of spiritual split personality like Dr. Jekyll and Mr. Hyde. You are righteous to the core!

Don't allow what you feel or even how you may have behaved to determine what you believe about yourself. Allow *God* to have the last word on the subject of your identity. The Bible plainly teaches that the old nature that was passed on to us by Adam died with Jesus Christ. It is therefore a lie that you need to feed the new man and starve the old man, because that old man is already dead—and dead men don't eat anything. The truth of the Bible is that you have the nature of Jesus Christ, and that is your one, single nature. Refuse to believe that, and you'll set yourself up for constant internal conflict. Believe it, and you'll be equipped to live life out of the truth of your authentic self.

We Need to Seek Spiritual Power

The desire to experience divine power in our daily lives is admirable. Most Christians have been taught about the importance of the power of the Holy Spirit at work in our lives. It's a teaching that has great value because we do indeed need the power of Christ to live the lifestyle that our Father has purposed for us.

There is no question about the need for spiritual power in our lives. The issue in the lie that we need to seek spiritual power concerns the matter of seeking it. Do we need to seek power from God? The New Testament says that we do not. We already have the power of God in our lives because of the presence of His indwelling life within us.

As a young pastor, I spent countless hours pursuing the power of God. I thought that if I did enough praying, fasting, and Bible studying (proving my sincerity with my actions), then maybe—just maybe—I'd be able to gain the power I wanted in my life.

The tragedy in my approach is that I didn't realize that I already possessed the very power I was trying to gain through my zealous attempts. The idea that we need to seek spiritual power has caused many Christians to pursue the power of God for their lives in a relentless "search for something more." That sounds like a noble pursuit. When you run into people who are expending so much energy and effort in chasing after the supernatural power of the Spirit, you find it hard not to be impressed with their zeal. The fact remains, though, that no matter how sincere these pursuits might be, they are pointed at the wrong target. We don't need to seek spiritual power. We don't need more power from God. We simply need to discover the power we already have in Christ.

The Truth Is So Much Better!

Did you know that you have divine life in you at this very moment? You have the indwelling Christ inside of you. That reality has tremendous ramifications in your life. The Bible says this about Jesus: "In Him all the fullness of Deity dwells in bodily form" (Colossians 2:9). The complete reservoir of divine power is in Jesus Christ. There is not even one small part of supernatural power that He doesn't possess.

Now, consider this question: Where is Jesus Christ in relation to you at this moment? The answer is that He lives in you! You already have the power of God inside you. The second part of the statement about the fullness of Deity dwelling in Jesus is this: "In Him you have been made complete" (2:10). Because of Christ living inside you, you lack nothing. You have been made complete in Him. You'll find no *incompleteness* of spiritual power in you because He completes you in that area too!

Following the resurrection, Jesus said to the disciples, "But you shall receive power when the Holy Spirit has come upon you; and you shall be My witnesses both in Jerusalem, and in all Judea and Samaria, and even to the remotest part of the earth" (Acts 1:8). Jesus promised His disciples that with the coming of His Spirit they would receive power. The Greek word for power is *dunamis,* from which we get the English word *dynamite.* At this moment, you have the explosive dynamo of divine life in you. That means you have omnipotent power resting and residing in you at all times. That's why the apostle Paul could say, "I can do all things through Him who strengthens me" (Philippians 4:13).

In another passage, Paul described how he lived his own life based on the power he already possessed in Jesus Christ. He wrote, "I labor, striving according to His power, which mightily works within me" (Colossians 1:29).

Paul's lifestyle was characterized by hard work in the service of God through his service to others. It would be hard to find someone who ever gave more to the work of ministry, but how did he do it? He says that it was "*according to His power,* which mightily works *within me.*" Paul knew the secret of trusting the indwelling Christ. He knew he didn't need *more* power. He knew he lacked nothing. Paul knew that when Christ lives in you, you have everything you need. That's why he taught, "Blessed be the God and Father of our Lord Jesus Christ, who has blessed us with *every spiritual blessing* in the heavenly places in Christ" (Ephesians 1:3). "Every spiritual blessing" includes the power of God. He *has blessed* (past tense) us with His power. It's not something we have to seek.

Clarify Your Thinking

The idea that you lack spiritual power is a legalistic teaching because it causes you to think that you have to do something to gain it. The truth is that you have it. Stop looking for the power of God. It is in you—or, to be more precise, *He* is in you and will express the dynamic power of the Father's love and grace through you every day as you depend on Him.

You lack nothing. "Now to Him who is able to do far more abundantly beyond all that we ask or think, *according to the power that works within us,* to Him be the glory in the church and in Christ Jesus to all generations forever and ever. Amen" (Ephesians 3:20-21)!

Lie #35

We Should
Live by
Christian Morals

Here's one that might surprise a lot of people. Who can be against living by Christian morals? Shouldn't we live morally as opposed to living immorally?

That question misses the point because whether we see people as living morally or immorally, we're viewing life through a lens we aren't intended to use. God hasn't designed life to be lived based on a system of morality. He has a much better plan in mind for us than that.

The idea of living by Christian morals raises some questions. What exactly *are* "Christian morals"? Which morals are specifically unique to Christianity? Being against lying, stealing, and adultery? What about honoring your mother and father, and treating your neighbor the way you would like to be treated? All the major religions of the world agree on these. There are even atheists whose moral code is essentially the same as much of what the Ten Commandments teach. I ask again: What morals are specifically Christian? Let's move on.

"Yes, I admit you're right," someone could say, "but Christians *keep those morals* better than members of other religions or nonbelievers." If you actually are naïve enough to believe this, I've got some acreage in the Florida Everglades I'd like to show you. Seriously, let's get back to reality. Those who build their lives around morality have the same chances of success and the same chances for failure. Our lives aren't built on morals, but on Christ Himself.

In Jesus' time, just as in our own, there were many people who were highly moral, according to human standards. To grasp what God wants us to learn about morals, we need to confront the fact that this was never His intent for humanity.

The Truth Is So Much Better!

In the second chapter of Genesis, the Bible sets forth the two alternatives for how we will live in this world. The tree of life and the tree of the knowledge of good and evil represent these two systems. Both were in the center of the Garden of Eden.

The tree of life represents Jesus Christ. We know that because of what the New Testament teaches. One basic principle in interpreting the Bible is that we understand the meaning of the Old Testament Scriptures based on the New Testament. We know the tree of life foreshadows Jesus. After all, even a casual reading of the New Testament shows that Jesus Christ is life.

The tree of the knowledge of good and evil is the tree of morality. Why would I suggest that idea? Allow me to answer the question with a question: What did this particular tree give to Adam and Eve? Knowledge. But knowledge about what? The answer, of course, is good and evil. So the tree provided the knowledge of good and evil—or, put another way—right and wrong.

Right and wrong are the boundaries for the land of morality. Moral living is entirely based on doing right and avoiding wrong behavior. That's the essence of morality. Do good. Don't do evil. It's that simple.

To study what God told Adam and Eve in the garden shows us His intent for how we are to live. He did not tell them that they could eat from the "morality tree" as long as they ate from the good branch but avoided the evil one. He told them plainly *not to eat from the Tree of the*

Knowledge of Good and Evil at all (see Genesis 2:17). God's plan is not that we should live our lives based on doing good things and avoiding evil ones.

Jesus explained the plan for how we are to live in John 15:4-5. He said, "Abide in Me, and I in you. As the branch cannot bear fruit of itself unless it abides in the vine, so neither can you unless you abide in Me. I am the vine, you are the branches; he who abides in Me and I in him, he bears much fruit, for apart from Me you can do nothing."

The clear plan described by Jesus Himself is that our lifestyles are to be an expression of His divine life flowing through us and producing fruit. It isn't a matter of moral living. We are capable of *miraculous* living as we trust Him as our very life source.

Clarify Your Thinking

You and I are capable of much more than moral living. "Christian morals" is an oxymoron. We aren't to live by morals. We are to live by the life of Jesus. The idea of living by morals suggests that we find out what's right and wrong, and that we focus on doing the right and avoiding the wrong. What that really means, then, is that we live on the tree of the knowledge of good and evil. That's not God's plan.

It's not even required that a person follow Christ to live morally. But we *do* follow Christ. We live by a life that transcends morality. We literally live by the life of another person. Our goal is to trust Christ and allow Him to be who He is, in us and through us. That is infinitely better than trying to be a moral person.

Lie #36

Your Heart Is Desperately Wicked

For many years I believed that at the core of my being, I was still a wicked person. I knew I had been forgiven, but still saw inclinations toward sinful thoughts, attitudes, and even actions. I had heard for most of my life that—although we are forgiven—our hearts are still wicked and untrustworthy.

The fact is that our hearts *aren't* wicked now. If we believe the lie that they are, we will find ourselves acting out of that wrong belief. We will act in a way that ultimately will fulfill what we believe. That's a basic principle of the human psyche.

I've often heard preachers say that we all are wicked to the core. They speak of human depravity as though the cross has meant nothing in our lives. But Jesus Christ is a greater Savior than many of us have even imagined. What He has done has brought about a change within us, and it is surprising to many people when they come to discover the truth about the matter.

Where does this idea that "your heart is desperately wicked" come from? You've probably heard that said many times and by many people. It is from the Bible. It comes from the Old Testament book of Jeremiah.

"The heart is more deceitful than all else and is desperately sick; who can understand it?" asked the prophet (see Jeremiah 17:9).

Did you notice the source I said they were quoting? They are quoting from the Old Testament—the old covenant. While the whole Bible is written for us and is profitable for our study and spiritual growth, not every word can be accurately applied to new covenant believers. It is vitally important to properly interpret the Scripture. That means we have to use proper rules of interpretation. In fact, a whole field of study called *hermeneutics* deals with that matter. Hermeneutics is the branch of theology that deals with how to properly interpret the Bible in a way that ensures intellectual honesty. There are many sound principles for properly understanding the Bible. Chief among these is *context*. That means in any passage you read, you must consider these questions:

1. *Who* is speaking or writing?
2. *When* were they speaking or writing?
3. *To whom* are they speaking or writing?
4. What was their *intended meaning* at the time?
5. Under what conditions were they giving their message?

When you read anything in the Bible that was written before the new covenant was ratified at the cross, you must interpret the passage in light of the fact that the message was given to people living under the Law. We can certainly *learn from* Old Testament Scripture, but it is also true that we must keep in mind that *we ourselves do not live under that covenant.* We live under the conditions of the new covenant, which was inaugurated at the cross, when Jesus Christ shed His blood on our behalf. Here's a key that will help you avoid misunderstanding the Bible: *All of the Bible is written for your benefit, but not all of it is addressed directly to you.*

Jeremiah's statement about the heart was true for the people to whom he spoke. These were old covenant people who hadn't yet had the privilege of experiencing the finished work of Jesus Christ on the cross. However, our God, being the gracious God that He is, promised that He was going to do something new about their problem.

The Truth Is So Much Better!

After the Fall of man in the Garden of Eden, man's problem became a heart problem. The heart of humanity was suddenly darkened with sin at the Fall, and no cure was available for our dead hearts. What we needed was a heart replacement. That's why, centuries before Christ Jesus came, God promised His solution to get to the source of the problem.

> I will sprinkle clean water on you, and you will be clean; I will cleanse you from all your filthiness and from all your idols. Moreover, I will give you a new heart and put a new spirit within you; and I will remove the heart of stone from your flesh and give you a heart of flesh. I will put My Spirit within you and cause you to walk in My statutes, and you will be careful to observe My ordinances (Ezekiel 36:25-27).

In this prediction, made about 600 years before Christ, our gracious Father gave a clear foreshadowing of what He would do through the person and work of His Son. You see the spiritual cleansing that the Lord would accomplish through His death, which was fulfilled in forgiveness, justification, and more. You see, more to our present point, that God promises to exchange man's heart. He will take away the old, hard, depraved heart, and replace it with a new, soft, responsive heart. To make sure that this change results in the desired direction, God said He would also give us His Spirit.

Now I ask you: If all these things have come true in Jesus Christ, how could my heart still be rotten to the core? It can't. Paul wrote, "But the one who joins himself to the Lord is one *spirit with Him*" (1 Corinthians 6:17).

This is a mind-boggling truth, and it has serious implications for our question. Because we have become "one spirit" with Jesus Christ, how could we remain the same as before? How could we still have a wicked heart?

Finally, Peter shares from his perspective: "By these He has granted to us His precious and magnificent promises, so that by them *you may become partakers of the divine nature,* having escaped the corruption that is in the world by lust" (2 Peter 1:4).

To be a "partaker of the divine nature" means that the very nature of God has become ours. Naturally, this doesn't mean we become God, but we have received His nature because we are now in union with Him.

Because of your salvation in Christ, you have been given a new heart. Your heart is not desperately wicked. Now the nature of Jesus Christ fills you. Jesus Christ is your righteousness.

Clarify Your Thinking

Don't ever forget that you are not desperately wicked. You are not evil to the core. You are not depraved anymore. Now, because of the finished work of Christ, and because of the gift of His life that He has placed into you, you're not depraved. You are not rotten to the core— you are *righteous* to the core: "Therefore if anyone is in Christ, he is a new creature; the old things passed away; behold, new things have come" (2 Corinthians 5:17).

This teaching that the heart is desperately wicked will keep you in bondage because it will cause you to believe that you can't trust your heart. And the truth of the matter is that you can trust the Holy Spirit of Christ who lives in you. He will guide you, and He will continue the work He began in you until you are completely conformed to His image.

You Need an Accountability Partner

I realize that I'm really getting out into the deep water with this one because I'm criticizing a strong current fad. It is in vogue now in the church world to teach people that they must have an accountability partner. But there are some real problems with how this is often understood and practiced, assuming your concept of it fits the generally understood meaning I've encountered in many places.

If you're not familiar with this concept, an accountability partner is usually the title for somebody with whom you meet every week and to whom you divulge your darkest secrets. You tell them about your greatest struggles, and they hold you accountable to make sure you are living in the right way and doing the right things.

The way this practice is promoted is that you are supposed to give your accountability partner a license to be hard on you, demand answers, and jump on you if you are falling short. You have to be truthful about your deepest darkest sins. You have to reveal anything and everything, from whether or not you read your Bible enough this week to whether you have had your quiet time or had dirty thoughts. You have to be totally *transparent,* which is the word you hear over and over. And remember, *transparent* literally means that you can see *everything.* This is one of the limitations of such a stringent setup: The value of an accountability partner is no better than your willingness to be honest with the person you are talking to. The reality is that only you and God will know the truth about that.

Now that may not be the way you think of the term *accountability partner*, but as I travel and speak in many places, that is how I often hear it presented. The matter I'm discussing here isn't the idea of having a good friend with whom you can be honest and who encourages you by calling forth the best from you. The essence of what I'm challenging here is *accountability*—giving an accounting of your behavior to somebody else who is there to examine you to see how you've done. Affirmation that helps you grow in your love for Jesus is a different scenario altogether. But here I'm describing a time where your behavior is judged by another person.

Here's the truth: You don't need somebody to police your daily lifestyle. You don't need somebody to evaluate you about whether or not you are doing the things you think you need to be doing. Do you hear the legalistic undertones of that? You might tell your accountability partner, "I must be avoiding this or that. My friend, I need you to put on a sheriff's badge every week and sit down with me, challenge me, and ask me if I'm doing those things or not. Hold me accountable. Otherwise, I'll do the wrong things."

Once you look at it that way, you can see that this is an extreme action to take. Now if you have a specific area of life where you are having trouble making a change—an area where you want encouragement—fine. Ask a trusted friend for help, because that will be an honor for a true friend. But to say I need it as a *lifestyle* because I can't live an ordinary lifestyle consistent with my faith is a sign that there are far bigger things wrong.

The idea of an ongoing accountability partner is just not a fit with the grace walk. Put this into perspective: We all need good Christian friends. The Bible has a lot to say about our role to help, encourage, and counsel one another. Maybe you have a person in your life you have called an accountability partner, but you don't have the kind of relationship I've already described. Instead, you have the kind of relationship where you meet together to encourage each other and lift each other up, and you pull each other up toward your best. If so, that is good! We all need to be encouragers, and we need encouragers in our lives.

The Truth Is So Much Better!

The common idea of an accountability partner is a cheap counterfeit of an authentic relationship based on trust and encouragement, and it actually gets in the way of our developing that kind of relationship. We do need each other. God has built us so that we are not meant to live out our lives alone. The New Testament speaks often about the positive effects we have on one another. For instance, Paul wrote, "Bear one another's burdens, and thereby fulfill the law of Christ" (Galatians 6:2).

On another occasion, he said, "Be devoted to one another in brotherly love; give preference to one another in honor…Rejoice with those who rejoice, weep with those who weep" (Romans 12:10,15).

To the Thessalonians, he wrote, "We urge you, brethren, admonish the unruly, encourage the fainthearted, help the weak, be patient with everyone" (1 Thessalonians 5:14).

The writer of Hebrews encourages us, "And let us consider how to stimulate one another to love and good deeds, not forsaking our own assembling together, as is the habit of some, but encouraging one another; and all the more as you see the day drawing near" (Hebrews 10:24-25).

I believe that if you read those verses carefully and notice their prevailing *tone*, you'll agree that they sound very different from the heavy-handed "accountability partner" concept. Ask yourself: Would you like to be the *recipient* of other believers' attention in the way those verses describe? Of course you would! Who wouldn't want to be treated that way? But the accountability partner movement comes across more like the secret police. It's simply Pharisaism in modern dress.

Is there ever a time when it is appropriate to correct each another or to tell each other when we're wrong? Yes, there is—assuming that we have the kind of relationship with each other that makes it a perfectly acceptable expression of authentic love. Paul described it this way: "And concerning you, my brethren, I myself also am convinced that you yourselves are full of goodness, filled with all knowledge and able to admonish one another" (Romans 15:14).

Yes, there are times when someone telling us we are wrong is an expression of love. If you're going the wrong way, it's a blessing and an act of loving ministry for somebody to tell us we're going in a dangerous direction. The Old and New Testaments agree on this. One proverb says, "Faithful are the wounds of a friend, but deceitful are the kisses of an enemy" (Proverbs 27:6).

However, no matter how much the Bible discusses the blessings of the help we can offer one another, the best truth of all about this is that God has already given us the best encourager possible—the indwelling Holy Spirit. Jesus said these things as He predicted the coming of the Spirit: "I will ask the Father, and He will give you another Helper, that He may be with you forever, that is the Spirit of truth" (John 14:16-17).

We have the Holy Spirit in us. We have the Holy Spirit to guide us. He is the one who will show us when we are not living up to who we are in Jesus Christ. He is the best accountability partner you'll ever have in life.

The word translated "Helper" is the Greek word *paraklētos,* from which we get the term *paraclete.* It means "one who comes alongside" to help and strengthen. It can mean a defense attorney or a counselor. That is the role of the Holy Spirit. Think about it: You have God Himself, that is, the person of the Holy Spirit—Christ's empowering presence—in you to counsel, teach, correct, strengthen, and help you. What a difference it could make if we were more aware of the resources God has already made available to us.

Clarify Your Thinking

Don't think I'm suggesting that it's not a good idea to have a friend with whom you are completely honest. I haven't said that, and I do not believe it. However, I do challenge the assertion that you need to answer to someone concerning what sins or vulnerabilities you may have (or whether you've done the right things). I believe that is a perversion of the biblical truths about the help we should give each other. And even more seriously, it can obscure the even greater truth that the Holy Spirit is your accountability partner. He will nurture and lead you, and encourage you onward and upward.

You Grow in Holiness

The way that a person is made holy has been one of the most hotly debated biblical issues in the church world for many, many years. Entire denominations have been formed over differences on this matter. The interesting (but sad) thing about it is this: These differences among people on this subject generally seem to arise from looking at the question from the wrong angle from the very start.

Ask the question, "How does a person become holy?" and you're likely to get many answers, but the answers will most likely all have one thing in common. They'll speak to the issue of what a person needs to *do*. Some people think we need to read our Bibles and develop a strong prayer life to become holy. Others think we achieve it by fasting. Still others think it comes from giving up bad habits and beginning to do the things we believe God would have us to do in our daily walk. There are many different answers people offer, but they all take the same approach. As with all legalistic views, it's all about what *we* do. As you've learned by now, grace doesn't run on that track. Grace is about what *God* does.

What does it actually mean to be *holy*? The definition of the word is "to be set apart by God." The idea is that the thing made holy has been set aside from common use and is now reserved for a particular purpose by God. That definition describes you! Your Father has set you apart for Himself and for His own purposes. It's not something you have done that caused it, but it is an act of grace that He has done in your life.

The reality is that you don't become holy by what you do, and you can't become more holy than you are right now. You have been set apart, and it's not possible for you to cause yourself to become "more set apart" than you already are.

The idea that you can grow in holiness is wrong on a number of grounds, not the least because it fails to recognize the finished work of Christ at the cross. The Bible teaches us that in Jesus Christ we have already been given holiness. The Scripture says in 1 Corinthians 3:16-17 that your body is the temple of the Holy Spirit, and that the Spirit of God lives in you. Verse 17 says that "the temple of God is holy, and that is what you *are*." You don't grow into holiness, and you don't gradually become holy. Holiness comes to you in the person of Jesus Christ.

Many struggle to believe they are holy because they often don't *feel* holy, and because they don't always *act* holy. We need to know that truth isn't determined by what we feel or how we behave. Truth is based on what God says.

You may not always act holy or feel holy, but that doesn't change the reality of who you are. Your identity is determined by what Christ has done, not by what you do. So your feelings and actions have nothing to do with the objective reality that you have been made holy in Jesus Christ. If you want to see your lifestyle changed, then apply and appropriate the truth of the holiness that is yours in Christ to your life, and you'll see a transformation come into your day-to-day actions and attitudes.

The Truth Is So Much Better!

If you think holiness has to do with moral perfection, I encourage you to take a look at the New Testament Church in Corinth. To say that these people misbehaved is an understatement. Inside that church existed divisions, drunkenness, jealousy, sexual immorality, and many other sinful behaviors.

The apostle Paul wrote the Corinthian Christians a letter, and he began it this way: "To the church of God which is at Corinth, to those who have been *sanctified* in Christ Jesus, *saints* by calling…" (1 Corinthians 1:2). Paul said the Corinthians were "sanctified in Christ Jesus." He knew about their behavior and even addressed it later in his letter, but Paul knew something that many believers today don't understand. *Our behavior does not determine who we are!* These Corinthians were saints, regardless of their behavior. They were saints, even if they were "saints behaving badly." Their holiness didn't have a thing to do with what they did or didn't do.

Paul reminded them a little later, "But *by His doing* you are in Christ Jesus, who became to us wisdom from God, and righteousness and *sanctification,* and redemption" (1 Corinthians 1:30). He says that it was *God's doing* that they were in Christ, and that Christ *is* their sanctification—or holiness. Again we see that the Corinthians were *already* holy in God's sight.

The New Testament Scriptures are very clear as to *how* we have become holy. The writer of Hebrews says that God did it through Christ: "By this will *we have been sanctified* through the offering of the body of Jesus Christ once for all" (Hebrews 10:10).

It is by Christ's work that we have been made holy. What about places in the Bible where the Scripture seems to teach that we are to seek holiness? Consider, for example, Hebrews 12:14: "Pursue peace with all men, and the sanctification without which no one will see the Lord." What does the verse mean when it tells us to "pursue" sanctification (holiness)? The answer has to do with what we mean by pursuing it.

If you define *pursuing sanctification* as getting better and better at keeping rules, you will find yourself right back in legalism, but we have already seen that rule-keeping is not the meaning of holiness.

To pursue it means that we act diligently to agree with God

concerning what He has said about us, and we act like it's true because it *is* true! You have Jesus Christ, and He *is* your holiness. So we are pursuing sanctification or holiness when we are living out of the reality of His indwelling life. We grow in the expression of holiness in our thoughts and attitudes and even in our actions, but we don't become more and more holy. You are holy. That is what you *are!* Remember 1 Corinthians 3:16-17.

Clarify Your Thinking

If you believe the lie that you must grow in holiness, there will be no other option than to start asking yourself what you need to do in order to make that happen. Believe the truth of the New Testament. You have already been made holy, and you'll find yourself becoming more and more motivated to live your lifestyle based on that truth.

Yes, we all find ourselves behaving more and more holy as we grow in grace and in the knowledge of who Jesus is in us and who we are in Him. That doesn't mean we are growing in holiness, though. It means that our actions are catching up with our identity. We are acting more and more like the person we already are.

The answer to the lie that we grow in holiness is to affirm that Christ Jesus *is* our holiness and simply accept His finished work as the basis for our holiness. When we do that, we honor the cross and the Christ who gave Himself for us so that we might be made holy.

Lie #39

You Should Pray to Love Christ More

For years of my life, I kept praying the same prayer over and over again: "Lord Jesus, help me to love You more." Have you prayed like that? If so, I know you have a hunger to experience intimacy with Him, and that desire motivated your prayer just as it did mine. To think that we ought to love Jesus more as we move forward through life seems reasonable. And if we ought to love Him more, we should pray to that end. That makes sense. Doesn't it?

I hope by now that you are recognizing the underlying common denominator in these legalistic lies. Look at the last paragraph again. What words did I write to tip you off that I was describing a legalistic approach to loving Christ? There are two words in the last paragraph that I hope jumped out at you.

I hope the words *ought* and *should* got your attention. By now I hope you realize that when our motivation in any area of our walk with Christ is *ought* or *should,* there is reason for us to pause and ask ourselves about the approach we're taking in our grace walk. As people living in grace, our motivation doesn't come from those categories. We have been brought over into the land of *want to!* It is desire for Christ that motivates us, not a sense of moral obligation. That's what grace does to a person.

Now consider how this applies to the subject of loving Jesus more. If praying to love Him more isn't the correct approach, then what is? The answer is so simple it might surprise you. Our love for Jesus Christ is a response to His love for us. It's not something that we initiate—we don't love Him more because that is what we determine we ought to do (or even pray to do). We grow in our love for Him as we grow in our understanding of how much He loves us. The Bible says, "We love, because He first loved us" (1 John 4:19).

So here is the question: Do you want to love Jesus Christ more? I'm sure you do, but the answer to that is not praying to Him to make you love Him more. The pathway toward loving Him more is to focus your attention on how much He loves you. As you focus on how much Jesus Christ loves you, you will become overwhelmed by His love, and you'll find swelling up within you a growing love for Him. You and I love Him because He loves us. He's the initiator, and we're the responders. When we reverse those roles and think that somehow it's up to us just to love Him more, that puts us in the driver's seat, and that's not what the Bible teaches. We love Him because He first loved us.

The Truth Is So Much Better!

There's an account in Luke 7 that illustrates this point. Jesus was invited to the house of a Pharisee for dinner. An immoral woman (or prostitute) in town "learned that he was reclining at the table in the Pharisee's house," so she "brought an alabaster flask of ointment, and standing behind him at his feet, weeping, she began to wet his feet with her tears and wiped them with the hair of her head and kissed his feet and anointed them with the ointment" (7:37-38 esv).

The Pharisee had a problem with her doing that because she was, after all, a sinner! What he was blind to was that the actions of the woman revealed her heart. She wasn't just pouring out ointment. She was pouring out herself before Jesus. You might say that she was professing her faith in His grace and goodness.

When the Pharisee complained about the inappropriateness of this vile woman even touching Jesus—whom the Pharisee must have seen as a respected rabbi—Jesus answered him with a story about a man who was owed 50 dollars by one man and 500 by another. Both men were broke, so the creditor decided to forgive the debt of both of them.

"Which one do you think would love the creditor the most?" He asked the Pharisee.

The Pharisee gave the obvious answer: "The one who had been forgiven the most."

"Exactly," Jesus said to him. "And that's what's going on here. I came into your house, and you didn't wash My feet, a normal courtesy to houseguests when they come in from the dusty road. You didn't even greet Me with a kiss on the cheek (again, a normal greeting), but this woman hasn't stopped bathing My feet with expensive perfume. She's been using her own hair since she came in! And she hasn't stopped kissing My feet!"

Then Jesus made the point that Pharisees never get. "The one who has been forgiven much loves much and the one who has been forgiven a little loves a little." Then He turned to the woman and said, "Your sins have all been forgiven."

Don't miss this important point that Jesus made. We will love Him more to the extent that we realize how much He loves us. Self-righteous people don't fully appreciate the great gift that God's forgiveness is to them. They think they aren't all that bad anyway. But those who understand just how much they have been given through the forgiveness of God are those whose love for Him grows by leaps and bounds.

Can you imagine how this woman, obviously believing that Jesus is the Son of God, must have felt when He told her that her sins were forgiven? No more guilt! No more shame! No more feeling as though God must be disappointed in her! She came to the realization that the

God of the universe had accepted her and loved her and that she was completely forgiven for a lifetime of bad behavior!

The same is true for you. Did you know that nothing wrong you've ever done, nothing wrong that you're doing right now, and nothing that you'll ever do wrong in the future will change how God feels about you one bit? His love for you will *never* be any greater or less than it is right now. He has demonstrated His love to you by the work at the cross. His love for you has *nothing* to do with what you do or don't do. It has everything to do with what a loving God He is! His love is unconditional, unwavering, and unilateral. He will love you forever and forever and forever. Nothing you've ever done or ever will do can change that.

Some people are afraid that if people really believe this, it will cause them to want to go out and sin, but that is absolutely untrue. The love of God expressed to us through His complete forgiveness doesn't diminish but inflames our love for Him.

Clarify Your Thinking

The secret to loving Him more is to let the reality of how much He loves you—which He has already proven—to take root in you. Think about it: Nothing will ever cause Him to love you any more or any less than He does right now. As you meditate on that truth, you will find love for Him gaining momentum inside you.

The teaching that you should pray to love Christ more is a lie that puts your focus on you and how much you're *not* loving Him right now. That will cause you to feel deficient and probably even guilty. It will cause you to feel as though something is wrong with you because you don't love Him more. Forget about that. Set your eyes on Him and pray like this: "Heavenly Father, I ask Your Holy Spirit to reveal to me how much You love me." As you pray that way, you will discover that His love for you will become a bridge that will lead you to a greater love for Him than you have ever imagined.

We Are Positionally Righteous

O ne of the most fundamental truths about our authentic selves and who we really are is often contradicted by well-meaning teachers of the Bible. The scriptural teaching that we have been made righteous through Him is not the least bit ambiguous. It's clear. By Jesus Christ's finished work, you have been made righteous. That is the starting place in understanding the truth about who you are at the core.

The challenge in accepting this teaching comes when we compare what the Bible says with what we feel about ourselves and how we act at times. Our feelings and actions would lead us to believe that, at best, we may be righteous some of the time but certainly cannot be 100 percent righteous 100 percent of the time.

This tension between personal experience and the plain teaching of the Bible leaves a dilemma. How can what the Bible clearly says be reconciled with what seems to be true based on personal experience? Here's where the lie that we are positionally righteous comes into focus.

The idea of *positional righteousness* is the teaching that we are righteous in a nonliteral sort of way. Proponents of the view will say that God *sees* us that way—righteousness is our position in Christ—but it's not an actual reality. There's a big problem with that viewpoint, though: *However God sees something is the way it is!*

God isn't playing mind games with Himself by telling Himself that we are righteous when we in fact aren't. Whatever God sees is called *reality!* If He sees you as righteous and says you are righteous, then you are.

To many, the claim that we are *positionally* righteous seems uncontroversial on the surface. At least it leaves the biblical teaching about who we are intact. It seems to be the perfect answer because it doesn't attack the integrity of what the Bible says about the subject and yet still leaves us able to explain how we can feel and act so *unrighteous* at times. What could be wrong with that?

The answer is that to suggest that the biblical teaching about our righteousness is only positional is actually a subtle way of *denying* what the Bible clearly teaches. To dilute the truth is to pollute the truth, and polluted truth is not truth but becomes a lie.

As is true with most of the lies addressed in this book, some of this misconception comes from people's honest confusion. They look at their lives and wrongly conclude, "I know I'm not righteous. I know how I act and how I really think and feel on the inside. There's no way I can literally be righteous." They mistakenly allow their own subjective experience to be the ultimate authority. As a result, they conclude, "I'm not righteous." Their problem is that they give more value to their subjective experience than they do to the objective truth of the Bible.

The Truth Is So Much Better!

The apostle Paul defined the finished work of Christ on the cross when he wrote, "He made Him who knew no sin to be sin on our behalf, so that we might become the righteousness of God in Him" (2 Corinthians 5:21). This verse doesn't lack any clarity at all. It plainly says that Jesus took our sin into Himself so that we could take His righteousness into us.

Did Jesus only *positionally* take our sin, or did He *literally* become sin for us? Does it make any sense to believe that He literally became sin on our behalf so that we might positionally become the righteousness of God in Him? The very idea is an illogical suggestion.

In his letter to the Romans, Paul addressed this matter so clearly that it's hard to miss that our righteousness is in fact literal and actual—not "positional." Continuing his comparison of Adam and Christ, he wrote, "For as through the one man's disobedience the many were made sinners, even so through the obedience of the One the many will be made righteous" (Romans 5:19).

Let's be intellectually honest here. If we were literally made sinners through Adam—if it isn't only a positional fact, but an actual one that we became sinners in him—does it not make perfect sense that in Christ we have actually and literally been made righteous? We can't take that verse and divide it right down the middle and insist that the first half is to be taken literally but the last half should be understood as less than literal. Either we were only positionally sinners and not literal ones in Adam, or else we are literally righteous in Christ.

Clarify Your Thinking

This distinction is so important because until we believe the truth that we have really been made righteous in Christ, we will be doomed to an underlying belief that to behave righteously goes against the grain for us. The truth is that to live a righteous lifestyle is completely compatible with who you are. To do otherwise is a contradiction of your true identity. You *are* righteous, and when you own that reality, you will find that this truth will empower you to act like it.

The suggestion that your righteousness is only positional and is therefore not a practical and real fact of your life is a lie. It will keep you from living up to your full potential as the righteous child of God you are. Don't accept a watered down, diluted understanding of your salvation in Christ. Believe it: You are literally righteous. Romans 5:17 says that those who "receive the abundance of grace and of the gift of righteousness will *reign in life*." That is reason enough to believe the truth and reject this lie!

Faith Requires that We Act Positively in Every Situation

Positive thinking has practically become a religion in Western culture. Whole bookshelves in stores are filled with books about positive thinking, with dozens of specific applications about how we can all see tremendous success if we'll just get our minds right. Many of these books and approaches are misguided in various ways, but few people would disagree that there are definite benefits to thinking positively as opposed to nursing a constant negative mind-set. I agree with that myself.

However, even though there are many aspects of biblical thinking that overlap and seem to agree with the popular philosophy of positive thinking, many of us haven't seen some significant differences. Some people have wrongly blended teaching about biblical faith with the trendy viewpoints of the positive thinking industry, and now they hold a mutant version of faith that is far removed from the pure meaning of faith as taught in Scripture.

Let's define *faith*. The Bible says that faith is "the substance of things hoped for, the evidence of things not seen" (Hebrews 11:1 KJV). Faith isn't empty hope or simply a positive confession of something we want to be true. Faith is the recognition of something that *is* a reality despite the fact that it's reality that cannot yet be seen.

John Darby was a Bible translator in the nineteenth century whose goal was to translate the Scripture from its original languages into English for those who had no training in the original biblical languages. His aim was to retain the exact meaning of the words the biblical writers used themselves. His translation of Hebrews 11:1 helps clarify the meaning of faith. It says, "Now faith is [the] *substantiating* of things hoped for, [the] conviction of things not seen" (DARBY). The substantiation of something is verification of something that is already real. Faith doesn't make something become real. It doesn't have creative powers. Faith is simply recognizing behind-the-scenes reality in the absence of empirical proof by human means.

So any talk about how faith "speaks things into existence" is unbiblical. Faith has no creative power in and of itself. What faith does do is affirm what already exists in the unseen world, and in God's timing, brings it into sight.

The widespread distorted thinking about the meaning of faith in some parts of the church today has led people to believe that faith means we have to always act positively. By that, I mean happy and upbeat, and saying words that reflect the way we want things to be whether they are that way or not. That's not faith at all. To other people, faith is wishful thinking. And yet other people's idea of faith borders on sorcery with an emphasis on reciting certain incantations (religious mantras) in order to manipulate the supernatural world to manifest the things desired.

"Christian positive thinking," often identified as faith, asserts that if you express *anything* that might sound negative—if you let it be known that you have negative feelings, if you express your uncertainty about the outcome of a situation, if you say anything that sounds even remotely negative about anything—then somehow you are not walking in faith. That is a lie. Faith doesn't require that we say ridiculous things that agree with what *we* want but may not align with reality as God has designed it.

One major problem with this lie is that it breeds an attitude of hypocrisy in the church. It makes people pretend, and it will not allow them to act in an authentic way. It leads people to act like they really believe something just because it's the way they hope things will turn out in a given situation. Or even worse, it causes people to fake it about their own thoughts and feelings. Allow me to give an example:

I remember attending a young man's funeral some years ago. The man had died suddenly and unexpectedly, leaving behind his wife. As my wife and I approached the widow, I collected my thoughts so that I might be of help and respond to someone in grief. But instead of expressing sadness, grief, or loss, the man's wife stood by the casket with an obviously phony, plastic smile on her face, and said, "I'm really happy. I'm glad he is in heaven."

I knew that, while the wife could certainly take comfort from the fact that her husband was in heaven, her whole demeanor betrayed the pain she had to be feeling. She was not glad he was in heaven *now.* Later, yes. But not *now.* Her husband had died. It was grotesque to watch this young widow act in such an unnatural way. What we saw wasn't real, and it certainly wasn't faith at work.

After my wife, Melanie, and I got home, I was still thinking about it. I facetiously said to her, "So help me—when I die, there had better be tears! You better be crying!" That widow was probably reacting like she thought she was *supposed* to react as a "spiritual Christian," but it wasn't genuine. Faith would have carried her *through* her grief without having to deny her grief over her husband's death.

The Truth Is So Much Better!

Faith doesn't demand that we pretend or fake it. It's not a matter of our becoming more effective actors. Faith means we trust that God is God, even in the middle of terrible situations. It is holding on to our knowledge that God is good, and that He loves us, no matter what happens. But pain still hurts, even if you're spiritual. Grief is still the normal human response to loss. People of faith still weep. Faith in God does not mean denying reality.

In 2 Corinthians 1, Paul speaks of being in Macedonia, where he had excessive burdens that were more than his ability to endure. He said, "We despaired even of life" (1:8). That sounds negative, don't you think? Paul had no problem using negative words to describe his emotions, and yet he goes on to say this all happened "so that we would not trust in ourselves, but in God that raises the dead" (1:9). There in the middle of discouragement and despair is Paul's expression of faith!

Paul doesn't avoid being honest about his true feelings in the name of faith. He doesn't put on a brave face and try to be "positive." The problems he faced were severe and deeply hurtful. It wasn't necessary to act positively in that situation. It was perfectly okay to act *honestly.*

One final biblical example is Jesus Himself. The night before the cross, He prayed and waited in the garden of Gethsemane. He cried out to the Father and sweated great drops of blood. He even prayed that He not have to face the cross at all—that He might not have to drink "this cup." The writer of Hebrews described that night: "In the days of His flesh, He offered up both prayers and supplications *with loud crying and tears* to the One able to save Him from death, and He was heard because of His piety" (Hebrews 5:7). Certainly, if the Son of God could express His emotions to the extent of "loud crying and tears," then so can we.

Clarify Your Thinking

It is important to understand the difference between joy and happiness. Paul wrote, "Rejoice always…in everything give thanks; for this is God's will for you in Christ Jesus" (1 Thessalonians 5:16,18). Joy is the deep-seated pleasure of knowing that regardless of what our external circumstances may be, our Father loves us and is working all things together for our good. Even when imprisoned in Rome, Paul wrote to "rejoice in the Lord always." Those words may seem strange from a man whose very life was in jeopardy when he wrote them. He certainly wasn't *happy* about being imprisoned, but he still had joy.

Happiness is dependent on our happenings. Its source is external, but the source of joy is *eternal*. Our source for life isn't rooted in this temporal world but instead we find joy knowing that we are already seated with Christ in the heavens. For that reason, it is totally acceptable that we acknowledge negative feelings of unhappiness while still affirming the joy we have based on the reality of our sovereign Father over us, an indwelling Christ inside us, and the Holy Spirit leading us through whatever we may face.

Faith does not require that we act positively in every situation. Faith simply asks that we look to the One who is in charge of all things and trust Him, knowing that whatever the outcome of our circumstance is, it's going to be okay; because He loves us, He is sovereign, and He has it all worked out. In times when He has given us clear knowledge of His desired outcome, we can speak with boldness about the situation. At times when we aren't clear about His purpose in our circumstances, we don't have to act and talk positively for fear of not walking in faith if we do otherwise. We can simply affirm our trust in Him and His loving ability and commitment to resolve our situation perfectly. When we've done that, we have acted in faith.

Lie #42

Christ Empowers Us to Keep God's Law

The Law of God is one of the most misunderstood parts of the Bible. Some people believe that Jesus lives in us to equip us to keep the Law of God. "Jesus fulfills the Law through me as I trust Him," you may hear them say.

Truthfully, I used to teach this myself and have even written in earlier books that as Christ lives His life through us we will fulfill the Law without even having to focus on it. It made sense to me until I began to look more closely at what the Scripture says about the subject. (We are *all* growing in grace, even authors who write about it!)

The problem I came to see with this viewpoint is that it still leaves us in a relationship to the Law. It simply changes from a negative one to a positive one. What the Bible actually teaches, however, is that you and I have *no* relationship to the Law—neither positive nor negative. The Law has nothing to do with us.

It's important to understand God's original purpose in giving the Law. Reading about the early history of man after the Creation recorded in Genesis, you notice that for centuries there was no law given to the human race. Then God selected Abram (Abraham) to begin a new work. From Abraham, then Isaac, then Jacob and his sons came the 12 tribes of Israel. They go down to live in Egypt, as a result of Joseph's journey there. Finally, in response to the people's cries for deliverance, God selects Moses as His leader to take Israel back to the Promised Land.

There, on the way to Canaan, God calls Moses to meet with Him on Mount Sinai, and He presents the covenant known as the Law of Moses (Exodus 19). The many chapters that follow—through Exodus, Leviticus, Numbers, and Deuteronomy—spell out the details of what was also known as the old covenant, the constitution of God's relationship with Israel. That covenant stayed in effect until the new covenant was inaugurated by the death of Jesus Christ.

Why did God give Israel the Law? Many think the Law was given to squelch sin among the people, but the real reason was very different.

The Truth Is So Much Better!

For what purpose do you think the Law was given? Do you think it was given so that the trespasses in people's lives might be decreased? The apostle Paul explains why God gave the Law to Israel. He wrote, "The Law came in so that the transgression would *increase*" (Romans 5:20). That biblical fact comes as a surprise to many people. God didn't give the Law to stop sin among His people but rather to stimulate it!

What possible reason would He have in doing such a thing? It was so that the people would come to see their sinfulness and abandon the misguided notion that their own moral character would ever be enough to achieve acceptance by God. The basis of God's acceptance of humanity has never been our own goodness. But it has always been because of His grace.

By stimulating sin in the people's lives, the Law would cause them to see how much they needed grace. This was a perfect situation because Paul went on to say, "But where sin increased, grace increased all the more" (Romans 5:20). Man's sin increased, and God's grace increased. Grace could not respond to the sense of self-righteousness that trapped Israel—but it would overtake and overshadow their sinfulness once they saw and admitted it. That's how it still works today, even among Gentiles (non-Jews) who try to keep religious rules as a way of gaining God's favor. Although the Law wasn't given to the Gentiles, it will do the same thing to you that it was intended to do in the lives of the Jewish nation of Israel when it was given to them.

In another New Testament passage, Paul described the Law as a tutor that came to lead them to Christ so that they would be justified by faith (see Galatians 3:24). So the Law was given to Israel to show them their sinfulness and their inability to earn acceptance by God through works.

How, then, could we rightfully think that Jesus Christ lives inside us to help us keep the Law? Jesus Christ didn't come to help *us* keep the Law. He came to fulfill the Law on our behalf and to deliver us from the Law system altogether! Romans 10:4 says, "Christ is the end of the Law for righteousness to everyone who believes." We don't even need to keep the Law today because we have the fulfillment of the Law living in us, and He has taken us away from all that! Note that I didn't say we break it. I said we don't keep it. Again, we have no relationship to the Law whatsoever.

Jesus has no intention to help you keep God's Law, but that's not all. He also wants you to know that you make a serious mistake when you focus on the Law at all. Your focus is to be on Him, not a set of rules that you imagine God requires of you. Your Father has no rule-keeping requirements for you! Jesus has ended that whole system. The Bible plainly says that "you are not under law but under grace" (Romans 6:14) and that "now we have been released from the law" (Romans 7:6).

Trying to live in the Law system is a misguided effort regardless of how sincere it may be. You don't have to *do* anything to earn your Father's acceptance. The Father accepts Jesus, and because you are in Him, you are as accepted by God the Father as Jesus Christ Himself! (See Ephesians 1:6.)

Sometimes those of us who teach of our freedom from the Law will cause critics to suggest that we are *antinomian*—a word that means "against the Law." My contention is that *they* are against the Law because they deny its biblical purpose under the old covenant and want to turn it into a moral code for living today. Trying to live by the Law is a curse because nobody can do it, but we don't have to do it! The Bible plainly says that "Christ redeemed us from the curse of the Law" (Galatians 3:13).

To try to live by religious rules today is to try to put yourself right back under that curse! The Scripture says, "For as many as are of the works of the Law are under a curse" (Galatians 3:10). So the lie that Jesus empowers us to fulfill the Law of God suggests that Jesus came in to us to put us under a curse!

Paul told the church at Rome, "Therefore, my brethren, you also were made to die to the Law through the body of Christ, so that you might be joined to another, to Him who was raised from the dead, in order that we might bear fruit for God" (Romans 7:4). Religious rules can never produce fruit. They only produce religious nuts! However, a lifestyle lived out of union with the Christ who dwells within us produces authentic spiritual fruit that honors God.

Clarify Your Thinking

If you've been taught that your relationship with God needs to stay focused on behaving in the right way, the idea that you don't have to live by religious rules anymore may be a little scary at first. Be assured that I'm not suggesting here that behavior isn't important. The truth is that if you want your behavior to honor your Father, it won't happen by trying to keep religious rules. In fact, the Bible says that religious rules actually arouse sinful desires in you. Romans 7:5 says that sinful passions are "aroused by the Law." Does it make sense that Jesus would empower you to focus on the Law when the Bible says the Law stimulates sin?

Our focus is to be Christ Himself, not a system of rules that we wrongly imagine God is expecting us to use as a code for living. Jesus is our *source* of living, and His life within us is more than enough to ensure that the actions in our lifestyle honor the Father. If we have believed that Christ empowers us to keep God's Law, we have believed a lie that will have the opposite effect in our lives than the one we want. Life isn't about keeping rules. It's all about Him—about living in His love and allowing that love to pour out of us onto others. The Law keeps us looking at ourselves and constantly judging ourselves for our failures. Grace allows us to stay focused on Christ and empowers us to express His life and love to everybody else. Which way do you want to live?

Lie #43

If You Don't Forgive Others, God Won't Forgive You

This is one of the scariest lies people hear today. Why? Because, let's face it, we have all needed to extend forgiveness to other people at various times in our lives but just didn't think we were ready to do it right then. If it's true that God won't forgive us unless we forgive others, then some people who may have been believers in Christ a long time could potentially leave this world without being forgiven by God. What would happen to them if that actually occurred? The question presents a seriously convoluted situation to try to resolve. They had trusted Christ, but they had been unforgiving in their hearts.

Not surprisingly, this teaching creates a lot of anxiety among Christians. The reason it weighs so heavily is because of what Jesus Himself said after telling His disciples how they should pray: "For if you forgive others for their transgressions, your heavenly Father will also forgive you. But if you do not forgive others, then your Father will not forgive your transgressions" (Matthew 6:14-15).

Those really are serious words, and they can strike fear into us if we apply them to our own lives. Take His words at face value, apply them to your life, and it would seem there's nothing to even discuss. How could we come to any other conclusion than to believe that our forgiveness totally depends on our forgiveness of others? The answer has to do with an important factor necessary to properly interpret the Bible. It's called *context*. To understand the Bible in the right way, we must consider the context in which the words were spoken. Verses must never be lifted out to stand alone, as if there's nothing else in the Bible. They must be interpreted in light of the greater context of the book they're found in with thoughtful consideration also given to the covenant under which they were written.

Jesus did say those words, but let me remind you again of the need to consider *when* Jesus was speaking and *to whom* He was speaking. Those are things you have to remember whenever you interpret the Scriptures. Not everything Jesus said is to be applied to you personally. That's because everything changed at the cross. When you read the Bible, always remember this: The entire Bible was written *for* you, but not all of it was addressed directly *to* you.

For instance, do you believe that what old covenant Scriptures say about giving burnt offerings apply to you today? The Old Testament says not to plant two kinds of seed in the same field. Should farmers practice that now? One old covenant law says that a rebellious son should be taken to the edge of the city and be stoned. Should our teens be worried? There are many things in the Bible that teach us without it being necessary to apply the verses to us in literal ways. There are eternal truths to be learned from Scripture that aren't intended to be personally applied to how we live our lives or relate to our Father in this new covenant time.

The Truth Is So Much Better!

How do we know which Scriptures are intended to apply to us personally and which ones aren't? The answer has to do with understanding when the old covenant ended and when the new covenant began. When did the new covenant actually begin? Hebrews 9:16-17 answers that question: "In the case of a will, it is necessary to prove the death of the one who made it, because a will is in force only when somebody has died; it never takes effect while the one who made it is living" (NIV).

The new covenant began upon *the death of Jesus*. It didn't start at the beginning of the Gospel of Matthew. That's important to understand. The New Testament Scriptures begins there, but the new covenant itself did not start until Jesus shed His blood at the cross. So the last Old Testament prophet was John the Baptist. He appears on the pages on New Testament Scriptures, but he was, in fact, an old covenant prophet.

Jesus inaugurated the new covenant when He died on the cross. When the new was put into effect, the old covenant became obsolete as a basis for how God and man relate to each other. Christ's death ended the covenant of Law and ushered in a new covenant of grace!

On the night before He died, Jesus took the cup and passed it, saying, "This cup which is poured out for you is the new covenant in My blood" (Luke 22:20). Covenants in the ancient world were ratified by the blood sacrifice of an animal. The words Jesus spoke about the cup being poured out pointed toward the passing of the covenant of Law and toward the new covenant.

Jesus' death not only inaugurated the new covenant, but it also simultaneously brought the Law (the old covenant) to an end. The Bible says, "When He said, 'A new covenant,' He has made the first *obsolete*." But whatever is becoming obsolete and growing old is ready to disappear" (Hebrews 8:13). Before the death of Jesus on the cross, the old covenant was still in effect. From the moment of His crucifixion, the new covenant became effective.

Seeing this dividing line enables us to rightly divide and understand the Scripture. Jesus lived under the old covenant, so when He spoke, He often used the Law to do what it was intended to do—raise awareness of spiritual need among His listeners. Try to apply everything Jesus said to your own life, and you will find yourself feeling absolute despair. His words were intended to bring the Jewish people of His day to a place where they could see their own spiritual need.

When we read the words of Jesus recorded in the Gospels, we must keep this in mind. When Jesus taught, "You must forgive in order to be forgiven," He was magnifying the demands of the law in order to provoke people to understand their need for a Savior. After His death, everything changed.

Read the New Testament statements about forgiveness after the cross, and you'll get a completely different picture of forgiveness—a new covenant picture. We don't forgive to be forgiven. In fact, we are already completely forgiven! Paul wrote, "In Him *we have* redemption through His blood, *the forgiveness of our trespasses,* according to the riches of His grace" (Ephesians 1:7). There's no mention of our forgiveness being contingent on anything we do in that verse. We *have the forgiveness of trespasses.*

Paul assures new covenant believers of the same thing in his letter to the church at Colossae. He wrote, "When you were dead in your transgressions and the uncircumcision of your flesh, He made you alive together with Him, *having forgiven us all our transgressions*" (Colossians 2:13). Do you see that it is a past tense action and has nothing to do with our first forgiving others before we can receive forgiveness?

The new covenant pattern after the cross is always presented in the same way. We don't forgive to get forgiveness. We forgive others because we have already received it ourselves. Paul encouraged the Ephesians, "Be kind to one another, tender-hearted, forgiving each other, *just as God in Christ also has forgiven you*" (Ephesians 4:32). What was the reason they were able to forgive each other? It's because Christ had already forgiven them.

Another example of this new covenant approach to forgiveness is found in Colossians 3:12-13: "So, as those who have been chosen of God, holy and beloved, put on a heart of compassion, kindness, humility, gentleness and patience; bearing with one another, and forgiving each other, whoever has a complaint against anyone; *just as the Lord forgave you, so also should you.*" Paul told them to forgive "just as the Lord forgave you," not "so *that* the Lord will forgive you."

Do you see the distinction there? Before the cross, the Bible says you forgive to be forgiven. But after the cross, the Scripture teaches that we forgive because we *have been* forgiven. The difference is because the old covenant is obsolete and we now live under a new covenant.

Clarify Your Thinking

The idea that if you don't forgive others God won't forgive you is an old covenant teaching, even though we hear it from the lips of Jesus. It was prior to the cross, which is where the rule of the Law ended. It's important to remember why He taught that and to remember who He said it to at that time. Things have changed now. By His death, burial, and resurrection, He accomplished the work, and the good news of the new covenant is now preached in His name.

Today, to tell someone that God won't forgive you if you don't forgive others is a lie. That's not applicable in the new covenant. The truth is, we forgive others because we have been forgiven. It's when we understand our complete forgiveness that we are able to extend the same to others.

Lie #44

You Shouldn't Do Anything that Might Offend Somebody

Because of some people's bias when they read the Bible, some of its teachings have morphed into ideas that don't even remotely resemble what it actually says. This is one of them. To suggest that we should never do anything that risks being offensive to anybody sounds kind and thoughtful at first. In fact, it almost sounds gracious, but to suggest that our behavior should *always* be regulated by what somebody else might think doesn't fit New Testament teaching at all. To insist that grace demands living that way is to ignore the fact that even Jesus didn't always choose His actions on the basis of who might be offended by them. Jesus often offended people, especially self-righteous ones. If never offending anyone is the mark of living up to what God expects, then even Jesus wouldn't qualify.

We don't have to build our lives around meeting the expectations of legalistic judges who seek to impose their religious regiment on us. Jesus didn't do that with the Pharisees or Sadducees. Paul didn't do it with the Judaizers, and he even rebuked Peter once when he altered his actions to appease visiting legalists. (See Galatians 2:11-21.)

So how then are we to regard this whole idea of being "a stumbling block"? It is in Romans 14 that we are cautioned about this matter.

Many Christians have been put into bondage by faulty teaching based on this passage. Some have drawn from that text the suggestion that if anything that you might do could potentially be offensive to somebody else, then you ought not to do it.

But think it through: If the Bible is really saying you and I should never do anything that someone might object to, then we will live in total bondage throughout life. We won't be free to do anything! There are a lot of people in this world, and there will be many expectations placed on us by other people as to how they want us to behave. If we have to live our lives constantly worrying about every single thing we do and how it will affect what those people think, we will become slaves to public opinion. There has to be something wrong with that idea.

The Truth Is So Much Better!

A discussion on the subject in the Bible can be found in these verses: "Therefore let us not judge one another anymore, but rather determine this—not to put an obstacle or stumbling block in a brother's way… It is good not to eat meat or to drink wine, or to do anything by which your brother stumbles" (Romans 14:13,21).

As we have seen so many times, these verses quoted in isolation seem to support the lie I'm challenging. However, if we carefully follow Paul's teaching in this section of Romans, we'll come to other conclusions. The passage is too long to quote entirely, but I can give you the outline of his reasoning.

Up to this chapter in the book of Romans, Paul has shared the longest and most systematic presentation of Christian doctrine in the Bible. Throughout his teaching from the first chapter, there has been a consistent underlying concern, which is to address both the Jewish Christians and Gentile Christians in the Roman church. Paul is deeply concerned with promoting unity in the church, particularly between these two groups. That was not an easy task.

Think of all the things that divided Jews and Gentiles. First, dietary laws, strictly regulating what Jews could and could not eat. Meat from a pig, shellfish, and catfish were out. Even the foods they could eat had to be prepared in specific ways.

Second, observance of the Sabbath, strictly regulating Jewish activities from sundown Friday to sundown Saturday, particularly the command to refrain from working. Third, the Jewish believers had been taught growing up that Gentiles were "unclean dogs" and that associating with them would cause defilement.

The Gentile believers grew up with no restrictions corresponding to these rules. Their "anything goes" lifestyles were disgusting and barbaric to the Jews. Yes, these Jews may have become Christians, but that did not instantly erase all those years of their disciplined practices or the now-involuntary emotional reactions they had to Gentile practices. In other words, they wouldn't have any desire to go and buy a nice pork chop at the market. It just wasn't in their frame of reference.

Now Paul has the challenge of getting those two groups together in Christian unity! He wants them to have fellowship with each other, which is primarily expressed in sharing meals together. How is he going to do it? That's what chapters 14 and 15 of Romans are all about. Here are his main points before the verses in question:

1. Do not judge the person who is "weak in faith" (14:1). This is likely directed toward a Gentile believer who is making fun of a Jewish Christian for keeping the old restrictions regarding food and the Sabbath.

2. Each individual is responsible to develop his own conviction before God regarding these matters (14:5). That's critically important because of the third item.

3. Remember—you only have to answer for your own actions, not those of someone else (14:10). For that reason, stop judging people who have different ideas and practices than you.

This is where the Gentile Christian, the "stronger brother" in this context, can go wrong. Based on his knowledge that the law is done away, he might badger and persuade the Jewish Christian to eat what he believes to be wrong. In so doing, the Gentile believer would be serving as a stumbling block. Paul wrote, "But he who doubts is condemned if he eats, because his eating is not from faith; and whatever is not from faith is sin" (Romans 14:23). The key in our actions is that we are to live in faith. Otherwise, whatever actions we might take come from the wrong perspective.

This is the true application of the stumbling block principle. It isn't about who's "right" or about the "right" interpretation of the rules. *It's about loving your brother.* It's about loving your brother enough to limit your application of freedom for the time being in order to be considerate of the other's conscience. "For if because of food your brother is hurt, you are no longer walking according to love. Do not destroy with your food him for whom Christ died" (Romans 14:15).

If you truly understand your freedom in Christ and are motivated by love, then Paul's instruction makes perfect sense. "Now we who are strong ought to bear the weaknesses of those without strength, and not just please ourselves" (Romans 15:1).

If we would follow Paul's teaching in this great passage, we would be able to maintain Christian unity, even though we differ on dozens of relatively unimportant issues. That's why he concludes his argument with this: "Therefore, accept one another, just as Christ also accepted us to the glory of God" (Romans 15:7).

The Bible teaches that we are to relate to each other on the basis of love. If we have a weaker brother in our lives who does not understand our freedom in Christ, then we ought to be cautious about our use of freedom. Because of our love for that brother, we might choose to voluntarily limit ourselves so as not to offend the person. That's an act of love, an act of grace toward a weaker brother—someone who's not strong in grace. It is not a license for teachers to order us to refrain from practices the Bible gives us freedom to do.

Clarify Your Thinking

If you look across the body of Christ, you will discover diverse opinions. We discuss a lot of things about which we differ, from how we dress to where we go and what we do. We discuss things like the use of alcohol, where it's okay to go, places we should avoid, which forms or entertainment are acceptable, and which are unacceptable. Some parts of the body of Christ discuss where we should shop. I spoke to somebody the other day who told me they believe that Christians ought not to shop at Wal-Mart because of what this person believes are unfair labor practices. That is a Christian conviction that they have. Fine, but does that mean I should never shop at Wal-Mart out of fear that I may offend that person?

The bottom line is this: To say that you shouldn't do anything that might offend somebody is a lie. You need to relate to every person in love, knowing that Jesus Himself sometimes offended religious people by the things He chose to do. He healed on the Sabbath. He said things they didn't like. So we relate to people from a heart of love, but we don't allow ourselves to be controlled by public opinion. You are free in Christ. Be willing to limit your freedom for the sake of a weaker brother or to promote unity, but never give an inch to a Pharisee, the legalist who wants to make rules for other people to obey.

God Needs You to Accomplish His Work

Here's another one I taught for many years when I served as a local church pastor. I would say things like, "You're the only hands the Lord has." I used that to motivate people to go and do and be what I believed the Bible teaches they should. For instance, I taught, "You're the only mouth God has. He needs you to be a witness for Him. So if you don't evangelize, who's going to do it?" "You are His feet," I'd say. "If you don't go, who will?"

At first hearing, that seems to be true. We might reason that the Lord is in heaven. The church is His body on the earth, and the body of Christ needs to do the work of Christ. If we don't share the gospel, who will? If we don't help the poor in Jesus' name, who will? If we don't give to support missions, ministries, and churches, who will? These truly are our responsibilities. It all sounds so correct, but...

The Bible makes it very clear that God doesn't need us. Jesus showed us that. One time when people worshiped Him, the Pharisees protested. Jesus replied, "I tell you, if these become silent, the stones will cry out!" (Luke 19:40). God doesn't even *need* our worship. Rocks could do it if He so chose. All things are God's, and He isn't dependent on human beings to accomplish anything He wants done.

To urge others to participate in this mission to serve Christ's purposes on earth is certainly legitimate. When understood properly, we will realize that joining Him in His work in this world is His gift to us. We cross the line, however, when we begin to view God as actually in need of our help. While it may appeal to the heroic types who want to make their mark for God, it is very dangerous for us to take on such a burden.

I'm not proud to admit the approach I took in my own preaching when I was a legalistic pastor. I could cite many examples, but I'll share one in the area of evangelism to illustrate my point. When I wanted to motivate the church about evangelism, this text was always good to get the job done.

It's a passage where the Lord commanded the prophet Ezekiel to preach to Israel regarding the coming judgment: "When I say to the wicked, 'You will surely die,' and you do not warn him or speak out to warn the wicked from his wicked way that he may live, that wicked man shall die in his iniquity, but his blood I will require at your hand" (Ezekiel 3:18).

Ignoring its specific historical meaning, I had built my message around applying my own faulty interpretation of that verse to Christians today. "If you don't preach the gospel to your lost family members and neighbors, they may go to hell. And their blood will be on your hands!" By the time I finished preaching, half the church was in shock and tears. They were ready to charge out and change the world.

There's certainly nothing wrong with being motivated about sharing the gospel with people if it's for the right reason, but to think God *needs* us to do it is out of bounds. He *allows* us to proclaim the gospel. In fact, when we understand the truth of the gospel, it would take God to *stop* us from telling the good news that has transformed our lives. That's very different from the idea that He needs us, don't you think?

The Truth Is So Much Better!

What if we are unwilling to do God's work? Is He stuck? If He actually needed us, He would be. There's a great story in Numbers 22.

Balak, a pagan king, hired a corrupt prophet named Balaam to curse Israel. However, God had other plans. When Balaam got to a certain point on his journey, he found that the donkey he was riding on refused to keep going. The animal finally lay down under him.

Balaam became furious and beat the donkey with his stick. "And the LORD opened the mouth of the donkey, and she said to Balaam, 'What have I done to you, that you have struck me these three times?'" (Numbers 22:28).

Eventually, Balaam's eyes were opened to see a fearsome angel standing in front of him with a drawn sword. He finally understood that the donkey had saved his life. So God can even use a donkey if that's what He decides to do!

God doesn't need us. He has angels beyond number, each of whom has intelligence and power beyond entire armies of men. He has the elements of nature, all of which are perfectly responsive to His will. Everything God created is standing by and available to be used by Him. Why would God be dependent on men? Rocks and donkeys will do if necessary.

Clarify Your Thinking

In Acts 17:25, Paul says God is not "served by human hands, as though He needed anything." No, God doesn't need you. That's a lie that's taught in church to manipulate people into religious activity.

The good news of the gospel is better than the idea that God needs you. God *wants* you. He doesn't want you because He's looking for a servant or a slave. He wants you because He is looking for a bride, and He wants to pour out His love on you. When we know that, we can move past the guilt that comes from thinking He needs us and that we're letting Him down. Finally, we'll be able to love and serve others from a healthy motivation instead of a legalistic one.

It's Better to Burn Out for Christ Than to Rust Out

Not all denominations have the same emphasis on service, but most in the evangelical world really stress the importance of zealous activity done in "Christian service." It often seems as though the single purpose of a sermon is to motivate you to do *more* and do it *better*. Traditional services in many churches seem more like pep rallies before the big game than anything else. The goal is to motivate and mobilize the membership to get out there and shake up the world for God!

It is within this sort of context in church that many of us have heard this lie come from other Christians: "It's better to burn out for Christ than to rust out." I made the statement many times from the pulpit myself...and I had many heads nodding in affirmation of the statement. Why wouldn't I find agreement with such a statement? Doesn't it sound noble? It sounds admirable that we would give ourselves to Christ in such a way that we would burn out for Him.

I used to think that I would like to spend my whole life serving Jesus Christ and burn out in the end, so there's nothing left to give Him. And again, it sounds admirable—so right. When I would call on people to come and commit themselves to that same level of commitment, they would respond in droves to do it.

But it's wrong. It's a lie to suggest that we'd do better to burn out than rust out, and here's why: God's plan for us is that we *burn on!* The idea that we should burn out instead of rust out comes from a mistaken notion that it has to be either/or. The lie fits easily with some personality types—particularly those that are naturally driven people. It's all or nothing to us. The problem comes when it's presented as if those are the only two possibilities. *Either* you burn out in service of Christ, *or* you rust out from inactivity. Who says those are the only options?

Our lives can be compared to the burning bush in which God appeared to Moses. Many people have written about this topic. (Major Ian Thomas is probably the most notable example. You might read his classic book called *The Saving Life of Christ.*) Our Father wants us to continue to burn on and on and on, fueled continuously and refreshed regularly by His unending life and power.

Certainly, we can get tired in the work of God in some ways. After all, we are human beings who live in physical bodies. Yes, we can get mentally, emotionally, and physically *tired* for a time. But that is *not* the same thing as being burned out. You can become worn out, but then you can find refreshment after a time of rest, recreation, and sleep. Being burned out is a different matter.

As strange as it may seem, to burn out in your Christian walk may be the best thing that could happen to you. It's a good thing if it brings you to the end of confidence in your own ability to manage your own life and causes you to abandon yourself to God's sufficiency within you. That's what He wants for us. But burning out is a bad thing if it causes us to stall out in our walk and instead live in a perpetual state of self-condemnation about the fact that we aren't doing what we imagine that we should be doing.

The Truth Is So Much Better!

By this point in this book, I hope you're able to apply insights and knowledge you've gained. Some of them touch on this issue. Consider some truths we have already identified that help define what genuine service of the Lord looks like.

We serve because we are *already loved and accepted* by God, *not* in order to earn His love and acceptance. Many, many sincere people have tried to serve God because they were trying to earn His love and acceptance. Not knowing about the righteousness we have in Christ, they try to become "worthy" of God's acceptance by driving themselves to do more and more and more. It is a futile and unnecessary way to live.

In comparison, listen to Paul explaining his motivation for the things he did: "For the love of Christ controls us, having concluded this, that one died for all, therefore all died; and He died for all, so that they who live might no longer live for themselves, but for Him who died and rose again on their behalf" (2 Corinthians 5:14-15).

Paul did not serve Christ because he was forced to do so. He wasn't trying to prove something to God, to others, or to himself by trying to burn out. He served out of the overflow of the love of Christ that flooded his own heart.

It wasn't because he was trying to be good enough to be loved. He wasn't trying to earn his way to heaven. It was the *love of Christ,* he said, that compelled him; that is, Paul's knowledge and experience of the transforming love of Jesus Christ. In effect, he was saying, "Christ's love and grace are so overwhelming that I can't help myself." Notice he didn't say that it was his love for Christ, but Christ's love for him that motivated him. Nobody will burn out who is motivated by Christ's love. That is the motivation that causes us to burn on.

Another reason why burning out for Jesus is a misguided goal is that it disconnects us from the means by which we serve. We don't serve Christ by our own determination or power. We serve according to the power of the indwelling Christ. Human willpower doesn't fuel our activity. God's power does that. Paul wrote, "For this purpose also I labor, striving *according to His power, which mightily works within me*" (Colossians 1:29).

One of the greatest causes of burnout is when we try to do the work of God by our own Christian commitment. We can rededicate ourselves over and over again, but ultimately human strength and resources will run out. On the other hand, the strength and resources of the living Christ never run out.

The works we do won't cause us to burn out because we don't manufacture godly works. They've been prepared in advance for us to enjoy. Paul wrote to the church at Ephesus, "We are His workmanship, created in Christ Jesus for good works, *which God prepared beforehand so that we would walk in them*" (Ephesians 2:10).

I've emphasized the last part of this verse for a reason. We don't have to adopt the burden of figuring out what God is doing all over the world and meeting all the needs. Remember—He doesn't need us. We just walk through the ordinary daily activities and discover the opportunities to serve that He has prepared for us. It really makes "ordinary life" a fun, adventurous experience when we determine to be on the lookout for these opportunities. Who knows in what fun and meaningful ways we can serve our neighbors today? People living like this do not burn out!

Serving God's purposes is *uplifting, nourishing, and fulfilling,* not a distasteful responsibility. Remember Jesus' experience? After an exhausting day, where we are told He was weary, tired, and hungry, He had the opportunity to share God's truth with the Samaritan woman. His disciples found Jesus reenergized and alert, and they wondered what happened. He said, "I have food to eat that you do not know about" (John 4:32).

We can know this experience too. We'll still get tired physically (and in other ways), but the energizing effect of being used by God and serving in His power lifts us up again. The Lord Jesus calls us into His "easy" yoke and His "light" burden, not the heavy burden of religion.

Many people who are sincerely trying to serve Christ have forgotten what kind of person He is. They act like He is a humorless, merciless taskmaster, cracking the whip and demanding our labor. They have forgotten what He said: "Come to Me, all who are weary and heavy-laden, and I will give you rest. Take My yoke upon you and learn from Me, for I am gentle and humble in heart, and you will find rest for your souls. For My yoke is easy and My burden is light" (Matthew 11:28-30).

Read those verses carefully. What kind of Lord is Jesus? What kind of load does He invite us to accept? Ask yourself this question: Would anyone get burned out carrying this burden? Would anybody living this way rust out? No, anybody who burns out or rusts out has been carrying some yoke other than the one Jesus gives.

Clarify Your Thinking

To say that "it's better to burn out than to rust out" is a lie. If you burn out, you're no better off than if you rust out. Either way, you're out! If *rust out* means to be lazy, inactive, and apathetic, then of course God doesn't want you to rust out. But neither does God want you to burn out. He wants you to burn *on,* as the apostle Paul confirms in 2 Corinthians 4:16: "Though the outward man is perishing, the inward man is being renewed day by day" (NKJV).

You Will Be Blessed Because You Tithe

Here's a serious hot potato! There are few ways more guaranteed to get people upset than to talk about their money. Even questioning the validity of tithing can get you into trouble in a hurry. But you and I are interested in truth as it is taught in God's Word, and we can't be afraid to question anything people say or do. Because of the sensitivity and confusion about this issue, I'm going to take extra space and time to answer it.

Tithing is taught in churches all over the world. It is almost taken for granted as truth, which is one of the reasons why people react so strongly when it is challenged. I'm sure most pastors teach it because they sincerely believe that's what the Bible teaches. But I also think we'd be less than honest if we didn't acknowledge that we Christian leaders have a vested interest in interpreting the Bible that way. Our need for money to support the work of ministry is a constant reality, and it can be a daily concern. Most of us went into the ministry to preach and teach God's Word and to serve in the advancement of His kingdom. Raising funds is, for most of us, a necessary but distasteful duty we often think we have to perform. So anything that makes it easier to do can be really tempting. I read once that when a person's income depends on him not seeing something, it will be very hard for him to see it.

I'm not saying anybody is being intellectually dishonest or has ulte-rior motives in what they teach. I'm just saying that we all look at the Bible through our own lenses, and sometimes we have personal reasons to see Scripture in certain ways. Certainly, when it comes to the matter of what's called "storehouse tithing"—tithing to the local church—there's reason to question our own motives and thinking so we can be sure that our viewpoint isn't influenced by our circumstances.

Let's make sure we know what the issue is. The word *tithe* means a "tenth" of something. Therefore it would be redundant to say, "I tithe 10 percent." The real issue is not whether people will benefit from giving a tenth of their income away in ministry (or if it is a meaningful practice for them). The question is whether or not we *have to*. The teaching I'm challenging is whether God commands believers to tithe. If He does, then those who don't tithe are living in disobedience to God.

Where tithing is taught as a command, this is the passage almost always used in support:

> "Will a man rob God? Yet you are robbing Me! But you say, 'How have we robbed You?' In tithes and offerings. You are cursed with a curse, for you are robbing Me, the whole nation of you! Bring the whole tithe into the store-house, so that there may be food in My house, and test Me now in this," says the LORD of hosts, "if I will not open for you the windows of heaven and pour out for you a bless-ing until it overflows. Then I will rebuke the devourer for you, so that it will not destroy the fruits of the ground; nor will your vine in the field cast its grapes," says the LORD of hosts. "All the nations will call you blessed, for you shall be a delightful land," says the LORD of hosts (Malachi 3:8-12).

The context is God rebuking the nation of Israel for her unfaithful-ness to the old covenant. The Lord spoke this message through Malachi, one of the last Old Testament prophets, around 400 B.C.

Let's take a moment to recall how Israel was to live. God separated one tribe, Levi, out of the nation to serve as priests and teachers of the people. From the Levites came the line of high priests who descended from Aaron. They were responsible for the formal worship at the tabernacle and temple. Unlike the other tribes, all of whom received a portion of the land, the Levites were distributed in cities throughout the nation, and they were forbidden to work as the others did (for instance, they were not allowed to farm). How were the continuous worship system and Levites to be supported? It was through the tithes of the rest of the people.

That's why the Law of Moses commands the Israelites to bring tithes of all their blessings to "the storehouse." The storehouses were literally places to receive the people's tithes of grain, fruit, wine, sheep, cattle, and so on, for distribution to the Levites and priests—to support the worship and sacrifices at the sanctuary and for the support of the priests and Levitical families. It was a very practical system. But this was a feature of the Law of Moses, the old covenant. And notice, there was nothing voluntary about it. The tithe for Old Testament Israel was no more optional than what you or I must give to the Internal Revenue Service when we pay our taxes. The tithe from Israel was mandatory, not an option.

As we have seen so many times in this book, we do not live under the Law. We live in the age of the new covenant, and the New Testament after the cross and resurrection is where we learn principles of living that apply directly to us.

I know somebody is going to say, "Now wait a minute, Steve! You're saying tithing is old covenant, but they tithed even before the Law was given." Well, that's true. Tithing was fairly common in the ancient world for the support of one's religion and to recognize one's sovereign. There is the well-known example of Abraham giving a tithe to the priest-king Melchizedek following his military victory in Genesis 14:17-20. This is how some teachers argue that, since this was before the Law of Moses, the principle continues after the Law of Moses.

But may I point out a few things? They also sacrificed animals before the Law was given. I don't hear anybody at church on Sunday insisting that we ought to be sacrificing animals today. God gave Abraham the practice of circumcision centuries before the Law, but I don't hear preachers demanding that today. Also existing before the Law were the practices of polygamy and levirate marriage (where a surviving brother must marry his dead brother's wife). So the fact that something was practiced before the Law means nothing in regard to whether the principle continues after the Law.

And one more thing: Did you know that according to the Bible, the tithe actually was not just 10 percent? There were additional tithes throughout the year. So if you add up all the tithes that they gave, it amounted to around 22 percent! So if they only gave 10 percent, they were still robbing God, according to Malachi 3:10. Is there any verse in the Scripture that's been used to beat people over the head more about money than that?

The Truth Is So Much Better!

The idea that we will be blessed because we tithe—or punished if we don't—is solidly an old covenant teaching. You will find *nothing* about tithing in the New Testament. Does that mean we are left without guidance for Christian giving? Far from it! The New Testament teachings on giving go far beyond tithing. Let me summarize them in the following points:

1. Giving under the new covenant is *responsive*. In the same way that the whole Christian life is motivated, we freely and gratefully give because we have first received from the Lord. "We love, because He first loved us," says 1 John 4:19. You could also say, "We *give* because He *first gave* to us." Those whose hearts have been touched by the amazing grace of Jesus Christ find themselves stirred with the desire to give.

2. Giving under the new covenant is *gracious*. Unlike the law of tithing, which was mandatory and specific, Christian

giving is *voluntary* and comes from the heart. It is absolutely not a command, which the Scriptures make clear. Paul urged the Corinthians to join him in giving to support the poor at Jerusalem, but he was careful to explain to them what he meant:

> Just as you abound in everything, in faith and utterance and knowledge and in all earnestness and in the love we inspired in you, see that you abound in this gracious work also. *I am not speaking this as a command,* but as proving through the earnestness of others the sincerity of your love also (2 Corinthians 8:7-8).

Paul said that, when it came to this matter of giving, he had no "command." The motivation for the Corinthians to give would be "the sincerity of [their] love." He even called the act of giving a "gracious work." It is a work of God's grace operating in us that motivates us to give, not an external demand to tithe. He wrote, "Each one must do just as he has purposed in his heart, *not grudgingly or under compulsion,* for God loves a cheerful giver" (2 Corinthians 9:7).

As you can see, this is totally different from the command to tithe, with curses or blessings tied to disobedience or obedience. And there is *no specific amount* Christians are told to give. Paul says each person should give "as he has purposed in his heart." It's between you and God.

3. Giving under the new covenant is *purposeful.* That means it is thoughtful and intelligent, and is aimed at specific objectives, chiefly two: (1) To advance the cause of the gospel through supporting people and ministries, and (2) to meet the needs of people, the poor, hungry, and needy.

To the first point, Paul says, "The one who is taught the word is to share all good things with the one who teaches him" (Galatians 6:6). To the second, Paul explains some of the positive results that happen when God's people give generously:

> The ministry of this service is not only fully supplying the needs of the saints, but is also overflowing through many thanksgivings to God. Because of the proof given by this ministry, they will glorify God for your obedience to your confession of the gospel of Christ and for the liberality of your contribution to them and to all, while they also, by prayer on your behalf, yearn for you because of the surpassing grace of God in you (2 Corinthians 9:12-14).

Genuine grace giving meets the need of people, motivates the recipients to honor God and give thanks, proves the reality of our faith, advances the work of the gospel, and builds unity and love in the body of Christ. What more reasons do we need? If you need one more, the Lord Jesus said, "It is more blessed to give than to receive" (Acts 20:35).

Clarify Your Thinking

The Old Testament tithe was a tax, not a gift. A lot of times today, people have that same legalistic attitude about giving. They think they have to give 10 percent of their income. They believe that if you don't tithe, your refrigerator will quit, or your car is going to need repair, or your kids are going to need braces. You know the kind of thing. They're really paying insurance premiums more than anything else when they give that way. Sometimes I've said that the way people pay their tithes, you would think they're being held hostage by God. They'd better pay up that ransom, or God's going to allow some bad thing to happen to them. What nonsense.

Others have said that the matter of tithing is a "revelation" that must come to you. If by that they mean that God's Spirit will reveal that everybody needs to give 10 percent, I strongly disagree. The Holy

Spirit won't reveal something that contradicts what the Bible teaches, and the Scripture teaches grace giving, not tithing.

Are we blessed when we give? Yes, it is a blessing to give, if you are giving out of faith and love for the Lord, and from a desire to do good for others in Jesus' name. But if you understand tithing to be a set amount you *must* give to be obedient to God, the answer is no. There is no blessing to be found in obeying a demand to give a tenth. The blessing comes from giving itself, just as Jesus said. The amount depends on what the Holy Spirit leads you to give. If you are giving in faith and love, you will be blessed for giving 5 or 8 or 15 percent. We give according to our ability. For some, 10 percent is currently impossible. Some may consider giving much more because of the abundance the Lord has granted them. Paul described it this way: "If the readiness is present, it is acceptable according to what a person has, not according to what he does not have" (2 Corinthians 8:12).

We live in a day of grace, and we practice grace giving. Do I believe in giving? Yes. Do I believe that we are to be generous in what we give? Yes. I can't imagine that grace will ever cause you to do less than legalism will. Now we're motivated to give because we love. We love the Lord Jesus Christ, and we want to give. We want to give to the work of the kingdom. We give because we've received the love of the Father, we have the nature of Jesus Christ, and it is our nature to give. I can assure you that grace will cause us to be more generous, cheerful givers, as opposed to giving grudgingly from a heart that is locked into the old covenant teaching of tithing. We give because we want to, not because we have to.

Lie #48

Sunday Is
the Christian
Sabbath

Many Christians grew up being taught that Sunday is the Sabbath. Not only did they have to "go to church," but they also needed to observe the day in other ways. Some wouldn't eat in restaurants on Sunday. Others wouldn't allow their children to play outside on Sunday. When I was a child, we were taught it was wrong to wash the car or mow the lawn on Sunday. There are still many ways that some people mark Sunday as a Sabbath day in the modern church world.

To understand this subject, it's important to clarify what we're talking about when we discuss the Sabbath. What is the Sabbath, anyway? Is it something we need to respect as new covenant believers? Do we truly have a holy day during the week we must set apart for special observance?

Among the peoples of the ancient world, only Israel had a Sabbath day. It was one of the Ten Commandments, and was specifically required under the Law of Moses.

> Remember the sabbath day, to keep it holy. Six days you shall labor and do all your work, but the seventh day is a sabbath of the LORD your God; in it you shall not do any work, you or your son or your daughter, your male or female servant or your cattle or your sojourner who stays with

you. For in six days the LORD made the heavens and the earth, the sea and all that is in them, and rested on the seventh day; therefore the LORD blessed the Sabbath day and made it holy (Exodus 20:8-11).

Notice some things about this requirement. First, it says nothing about "going to church" (or tabernacle, temple, or synagogue). It is a command to refrain from *working*. To make sure nobody found a loophole, the Lord made it clear that this meant everybody—you, your wife, your children, your slaves, and even Gentile strangers.

Second, the Sabbath day was what we know today as *Saturday*. But to be accurate, the Jewish people have always counted the Sabbath as beginning at sundown on Friday and lasting until sundown Saturday. Saturday is the "seventh day." Sunday is the first day of the week.

Third, the Lord was so serious about this command that violations of it were a capital crime: "Therefore you are to observe the sabbath, for it is holy to you. Everyone who profanes it shall surely be put to death; for whoever does any work on it, that person shall be cut off from among his people" (Exodus 31:14).

Fourth, notice that this commandment was for Israel alone. Nowhere in Scripture are any of the Gentile nations told to keep the Sabbath (except those living within the geographical boundaries of Israel). Neither are they criticized for not keeping it. This helps explain why the penalties were so severe: the Sabbath served as one of the most important "boundary markers" separating Israel from the rest of the world. It was quite successful at doing so. Other nations, such as the Greeks and Romans, found the Jewish practice of Sabbath-keeping hilarious and absurd. "How lazy those Jews are," they said, "who take a day out of every seven and refuse to work!"

The Truth Is So Much Better!

Even with all this Old Testament support, it is evident from the New Testament, and from the history of the early church, that Christians deliberately chose *not* to worship on the Sabbath. From the earliest records, Christians have gathered for worship and celebration on the *first day* of the week, which we call Sunday.

Acts 20:7 records an occasion when Paul met with and taught the church at Troas. It says, "*On the first day of the week,* when we were gathered together to break bread, Paul began talking to them." Note that it wasn't the last day (the Sabbath day) but the first day that the church met.

Another time, when he was gathering his collection for the saints in Jerusalem, Paul gave these instructions: "Now concerning the collection for the saints, as I directed the saints, as I directed the churches of Galatia, so do you also. *On the first day of every week* each of you is to put aside and save, as he may prosper, so that no collections be made when I come" (1 Corinthians 16:1-2).

Finally, we have the account of John's vision of the glorified Christ. It begins with this: "I was in the Spirit *on the Lord's day,* and I heard behind me a loud voice like the sound of a trumpet" (Revelation 1:10).

How did the early church get this freedom to no longer keep the Sabbath commandment, which had been so strictly enforced? The main reason, as we have seen so many times in this book, is because they knew that they were under a *new covenant* and that the Law of Moses was no longer in force. Why did they choose to worship on Sunday?

Most believe it's because Jesus Christ was raised from the dead on the first day. That's why Revelation 1:10 refers to it as "the Lord's day." Two thousand years later, although we rejoice in His resurrection every day, we still celebrate the Lord's resurrection in a special way on Easter Sunday. Even so, *Sunday is not a Sabbath.* By that I mean, God has not simply changed the day of the week while keeping the same requirement.

Spiritually speaking, the meaning of the Sabbath is that the work of Jesus Christ is finished and He is now our resting place. We don't work to gain God's acceptance. Because of the finished work of Christ, *all of life is an enjoyment of a Sabbath.* The Bible says, "The one who has entered His rest has himself also rested from his works, as God did from His" (Hebrews 4:10).

For the Christian, the Sabbath is not a day—not Sunday, not Saturday, not another day. The Sabbath for the Christian is a person named Jesus Christ. The Bible invites us to enter into the Sabbath as believers. Enter into Sabbath rest. Jesus is your Sabbath. It's not a day of the week; it's a life. Jesus Christ is the rest, the Sabbath for those of us who believe.

Clarify Your Thinking

So to suggest, then, that Sunday is the Christian Sabbath, is just an attempt to bring the Old Testament law and superimpose that on New Testament Christianity, and the two do not mix. The real Christian Sabbath is Jesus Christ. There is no greater rest.

If You Pray Long and Hard Enough, God Will Answer Your Prayers

Some subjects related to having God act on our behalf rouse up people in a hurry. This is one of them. So many people have been told for a long time that if they will just pray long enough and hard enough, God will answer their prayers. To suggest otherwise sounds like outright heresy to them. Others think getting God to answer them is not only a matter of the tenacity and length of their own prayers but also the number of people praying with them. Strength in numbers is their idea about getting God to do what they're wanting and asking.

I realize it's necessary for me to tread carefully here because it will mean stepping on a lot of toes. But I also need to be careful because it will deal with the hopes of many hurting people. When we have something very painful in our lives—a situation we ourselves face or a serious problem with someone we love—we tend to become desperate and grasp at anything that offers hope. Naturally, we want to cry out for God's help, and we do, sometimes repeatedly and many times daily. We understandably want as many other people crying out with us on our behalf. If enough of us pray, surely we can get God's attention and persuade Him to give us our request. That's how we often think about God answering prayer.

That's the reasoning behind prayer chains and prolonged prayer events. If we can get enough people praying sincerely and persistently around the clock, then we can get God to do what we want Him to do.

Don't misunderstand me. There's obviously nothing wrong with asking many people to spend a lot of time praying with you persistently about something. The Bible encourages us to do so in many places.

As I've written earlier in this book, not all Scripture was written directly to us, but it's all for our benefit. Even many passages in the Old Testament are very encouraging to us about God's faithfulness to hear and answer our prayers. The psalmist wrote, "As for me, I shall call upon God, and the LORD will save me. Evening and morning and at noon, I will complain and murmur, and He will hear my voice" (Psalm 55:16-17). Later he wrote, "I cry aloud with my voice to the LORD; I make supplication with my voice to the LORD. I pour out my complaint before Him; I declare my trouble before Him" (Psalm 142:1-2). Those are timeless truths. Our God's faithfulness is always reliable, and we can always bring our needs to Him.

Of course, our motives for praying aren't always that we think it will wear God down and cause Him to answer. Sometimes we pray about something because our hearts are filled with concern about the matter we're praying about, and we can do no less. I'm not criticizing that attitude. I'm rejecting the idea that great intensity or long duration of prayer is required to move our Father's heart so that He acts on our behalf. Those aren't necessary to cause Him to want to help us. His love is enough to do that.

Jesus once told a story that illustrates the heart of the Father toward us:

> Now He was telling them a parable to show that at all times they ought to pray and not to lose heart, saying, "In a certain city there was a judge who did not fear God and did not respect man. There was a widow in that city, and she kept

coming to him, saying, 'Give me legal protection from my opponent.' For a while he was unwilling, but afterward he said to himself, 'Even though I do not fear God nor respect man, yet because this widow bothers me, I will give her legal protection, otherwise by continually coming she will wear me out.'" And the Lord said, "Hear what the unrighteous judge said; now, will not God bring about justice for His elect who cry to Him day and night, and will He delay long over them? I tell you that He will bring about justice for them quickly" (Luke 18:1-8).

Isn't Jesus telling us all that we need to keep praying and praying and praying without giving up on the Father answering our prayer? I think this view misses the point. Jesus is using an *unrighteous* man as His example in this story. Jesus stresses twice that this judge "did not fear God nor respect man." He wasn't a loving, caring man at all. He was indifferent to the needs of the supplicant and had to be worn down by persistent begging.

The truth Jesus wants us to see is that we are not to think of God that way! In this story, Jesus was doing what He did so many other times, and that is to make an argument through contrast. We are missing the point if we think God is like that judge, unconcerned with people's needs and only responding if we badger Him into it. No, Jesus' point is, "If even an unrighteous, uncaring judge can be persuaded to act for you, *how much more will the perfectly loving and good God respond* to our heartfelt cries!" He isn't telling us that we have to pray tremendous lengths of time to persuade our Father. What He is saying is that any and every time you pray, you can have confidence that He hears and will answer. All the time you can pray, knowing that He loves you and isn't holding out on you until you prove your sincerity by time and effort in prayer. God isn't a judge who needs to be persuaded. He is a Father who is eager to answer you and show you His love!

We reverse it in our minds sometimes, and believe that God doesn't care. We think, "If we can just get enough people praying and log enough time in prayer, then maybe we can cause God to do something that He really isn't interested in doing. If He's not on our side now, maybe we can win Him over through sheer effort and persistence."

But the truth of grace is just the opposite. We don't have to persuade a reluctant, unconcerned God. It's the other way around. God is the seeker. He is the primary lover. God is always the initiator, so in reality, this is the way it works: When the Lord gets ready to do something, He often moves the hearts of His people to pray so that we might be moved to invite others to join us in prayer. Then they can share in the process and become a part of the answer as well. When we become involved in prayer, God allows us to participate in what He's doing in this world.

The Truth Is So Much Better!

Back to the story Jesus told of the unrighteous judge: It's important to note that in the story He told, Jesus had the supplicant appealing to a judge for help. He wanted us to see that our Father isn't like the person depicted in this story. The judge was reluctant to answer, but our Father isn't.

How we view God has everything to do with what expectations (faith) we have when we come to Him in prayer. I've already said that Jesus was using contrast to show the difference between our situation when we ask God for something and the situation of the widow in His story. There can be a difference in our expectation and approach when we come to Him because of the difference in the identities of the one the widow was beseeching and the One we are asking for help.

She was talking to a *judge*. You aren't. You are talking to *your Father*. That difference cannot be overstated. God isn't a Judge who is sitting in heaven with a judicial mind-set toward you that causes you to have to appeal to Him as you would ask a human judge to show you mercy and to grant your petition to the court.

Our God's relationship to you isn't judicial. It is familial. He is your

Father, and He delights in responding to our heartfelt requests. You can approach Him with the full knowledge that He doesn't have to be persuaded to act in your best interest. His role in your life is based on His loving character. That fact gives you reason to know that you don't have to beg Him. You don't have to get enough people to convince Him the way somebody might show up in court with a petition signed by a multitude of people to convince the judge to rule in their behalf. Your Father is already on your side and is eager to bless you in every way.

Clarify Your Thinking

Jesus said that we don't have to keep begging our Father for help. He said, "When you are praying, do not use meaningless repetition as the Gentiles do, for they suppose that they will be heard for their many words" (Matthew 6:7). Although they are sincere, many have done exactly what Jesus said not to do—they have prayed meaningless, repetitive, thoughtless prayers exactly as pagans do. Or they have prayed over and over and over the same thing, thinking that maybe God will finally take notice and answer.

I'm not suggesting that it's wrong to pray for something more than once or that it's wrong to ask other people to pray with you about the things that concern you. The purpose of this chapter is to address the lie that we need to convince God to answer our prayers by the length of time we pray or the number of people who pray with us. That's not true, and it is a dangerous lie that can make us manipulate God through that methodology. We don't have to do that. In fact, to do that at all is ridiculous. Our Father loves us dearly. On the basis of that love, we can come to Him and pray with confidence that He hears us and will respond to our prayers in a way that is in our best interest. A loving Father can do no less.

Lie #50

The Truth Will Set You Free

The foremost problem with this statement is in what it leaves out. To suggest that the truth will set you free is only a partial quote from Jesus Himself. What He *actually* said, in its totality, is this: "*You will know the truth,* and the truth will set you free."

Biblical truth alone has no ability to bring about any change in our lives. The Pharisees proved that. Although they knew their Bibles as well as anybody in their day, their knowledge of biblical content did nothing for them. To them, Bible study was an end unto itself. In other words, they studied the Bible *to know the Bible.* As strange as it may seem, that is a terrible reason to study Scripture. In fact, it can make a modern-day Pharisee out of you!

We don't study the Bible to learn its contents. We study the Bible to know its Author. It is only as the Scripture leads us into an experiential knowledge of our God that it has fulfilled its purpose in our lives. Remember that Jesus told the Pharisees concerning the Scriptures, "These are they which *testify of Me*" (John 5:39 NKJV). If you've found something other than Jesus Christ through Bible study, you've missed the point. Again, we don't study the Bible in order to learn it. We study it to learn *Him.*

The modern church world has taken the idea that the truth will set you free and has mistakenly believed that learning the propositional truths of Scripture will change us. Because of that viewpoint, they've turned the Bible into a handbook of religious guidelines. Ask them if the Bible is a book of guidelines for life, and most will say no. They profess to have a higher view of Scripture than that, but watch the way the application of Scripture to people's lives is made in sermons and Bible studies, and you'll come to a different conclusion about what they really believe.

There is often much application about what we are to now *do* that mentions nothing about knowing our Savior more intimately. Some may call this sort of teaching *practical,* but I think a better term for it could be *Christianity Lite* because its emphasis is so heavy on religious performance and so light on Christ Himself.

Unless they find a biblical principle of some sort and then show how that principle should guide our actions, many people think the teaching isn't practical. In reality, the demand for "practical teaching" in the church world today is a subtle mask for an underlying hunger to be *doing something* as opposed to *knowing Someone.* Certainly, nothing is wrong with understanding the practical ways that Christ wants to express Himself through our daily lifestyle. But people often teach biblical principles in such a way as to suggest that the aim of Christian living is to do right things. And nothing could be further from the truth. Remember, it's about knowing Him. All the doing will flow from that. When we reverse the two, we end up with nothing more than dead religious works, regardless of how admirable they may look to everybody around us.

We have not been called to live by biblical truths. We have been called to live by the truth, who is the indwelling Christ. He is our life source, and He animates our daily actions, not religious determination to act on information we might have learned. After I have shared a message from the Bible that focuses on Jesus Christ, sometimes somebody tells me that they wished the message had been more practical. When this happens, I inwardly shudder. Where did we ever get the idea that telling people what to do is a better way to teach the Bible than showing them who their God is? Jesus came to reveal the Father to us, not to tell us how to live. If that was *His* purpose in the world, doesn't it seem reasonable to argue that it's a good purpose statement for those who profess to follow Him?

Many people think that if we build our lives around biblical principles, then we'll experience the life God intends for us. As a result, we design a multitude of religious programs to help us learn the content of the Bible. We are largely a generation of Christians who think that the better we learn the Bible, the better life will be. "Christian education" has become a matter of memorizing Scripture at the novice end of the spectrum and parsing Greek verbs at the advanced end. But if that's the only thing that has happened, the result is a person who has some degree of Bible education but still hasn't been set free to really live. *Studying the Bible is not enough. We must engage with the Spirit of Christ through the Scripture to find real freedom.*

The ultimate truth of the Bible is Christ Jesus. He said, "I am...*the truth*" (John 14:6). Knowing biblical content can actually be harmful if it doesn't strengthen our knowledge of Jesus. Paul wrote that "knowledge puffs up" (1 Corinthians 8:1). It leads to arrogance rather than love.

The Truth Is So Much Better!

Jesus said, "*I am* the way, and *the truth,* and the life" (John 14:6). He is the One who sets us free. Biblical truth points us to the ultimate truth, which is Him. He alone is the One who can free us to live the life our creator intends for us to enjoy. That life flows from the union we share with our triune God. Jesus is "the way" we are to enjoy "the life" by living experientially in "the truth," which means to consciously live with the knowledge that He is our very life source.

Substituting *truth* with a small *t* for Jesus Christ is to take teachings of the Bible and try to apply them to our lives as a moral compass for our behavior. If unbelievers say they like Jesus but only apply the moral teachings He gives to their lives, we often see the folly in such an approach. But the same is true when believers approach the Bible that way. It is only when we encounter the *Truth* with a capital *T* (which is Jesus Christ Himself) that we will know Him firsthand. Only then does the truth transform us and set us free.

When Jesus said, "You shall *know* the truth and the truth shall set you free," He used the Greek word *ginōskō*. It is the same word used in Matthew 1:25 when the Bible says that Joseph "*knew* her [Mary] not till she had brought forth her firstborn son" (KJV).

Obviously, Joseph was acquainted with Mary before Jesus was born. The word *knew* means much more than that in the verse. The word was used as a Jewish idiom for physical intimacy with another person. It's interesting that Jesus used the same word when He spoke of knowing the truth that the Bible uses about Joseph and his intimate relationship to Mary. Jesus was indicating that truth alone will not set you free, but it is by an intimate knowledge of the truth that we are set free.

Clarify Your Thinking

The truth will set nobody free until they connect to the living truth (Jesus Christ) by faith. The truth is more than biblical *facts*. I've met *unbelievers* who proudly assert that they know the Bible very well. When it comes to propositional facts taught in Scripture, they have it down pat. However, eternal truth is personified in Christ, and by knowing Him, we are set free from the lies about ourselves, our lives, others, and even God.

Don't make the mistake of thinking that you will find freedom in your life by simply knowing the Bible better. The sterile propositional truths you may think you've found there will prove to be nothing more than accurate facts that won't change a thing in your life. On the other hand, by intimately knowing the One who is the truth of the Father expressed to us, you will know that truth, and *He* certainly will set you free.

Lie #51

You Must
Forgive
and Forget

S o many of these lies seem to have an element of truth in them. In
many cases, the statements have just enough "poison" to contami-
nate our minds with ideas that aren't biblical. This mixture of truth and
error often leaves people confused, and they sense that something isn't
right with their perspective. But they are unable to identify where the
problem lies, so they hang on to the lie and keep on futilely attempting to apply it to their lives in hopes that it will produce a positive outcome. Poison, however, can never make anybody healthy, regardless of
how small the dose may be.

The lie we're considering in this chapter is a perfect example. On
the surface, it sounds as though there couldn't possibly be anything
wrong with suggesting that we must forgive and forget when it comes
to offenses committed against us. After all, isn't forgiveness "the Christian way"? How could anybody dispute that idea?

As is true with most of the lies we've examined, this one has a number of underlying implications that undermine and negate the pure
truth that it contains. The pure truth in this case is that when we know
the forgiveness we have received from our Father through Christ, we
will forgive those who have hurt us. It's in our nature to do that, and

we will realize that once we've come to understand our own complete forgiveness by Him.

Will we *forget* the wrong done to us? Of course not. It would be ridiculous to think that the Bible teaches us that we have to have amnesia regarding certain experiences in our lives. Forgiving somebody may mean a lot of things, but it certainly doesn't mean that we literally forget what has happened. Not even God does that.

What does forgiving another person mean? A good working definition of *forgiveness* is this: Forgiveness is the intentional choice to release a person from all obligation they may have toward me as a result of any offense they have committed against me.

Notice that forgiveness isn't a feeling. It's a choice. Some may wonder, "Isn't forgiving somebody when I don't really feel like it hypocritical?" Absolutely not! We don't determine our actions based on our feelings. Our faith in Christ governs our decisions, not how we feel. It's *not* hypocritical to rise above our emotions and act in a way that is consistent with our Christian character! Feelings are incidental to the whole matter.

Why do we forgive? It's not primarily for the sake of the other person, but for our own sake. In Isaiah 43:5, God said, "I, even I, am the one who wipes out your transgressions *for My own sake.*" It's the nature of our loving God to forgive, and that's why He has done it. God would have been inconsistent if He hadn't forgiven you. After all, He is a forgiving God by nature.

Despite what we may feel when we consider the wrongs committed against us, it is our nature to forgive too. It's our nature because we have received our Father's nature within us (see 2 Peter 1:4). We forgive others because His nature is within us and to do any less is to act in a way that is contrary to our authentic selves. We forgive for our own sakes so that we won't be poisoned by bitterness that grows in the absence of forgiveness.

It's not an issue that we *must* forgive others. When we understand the fullness of the forgiveness that we ourselves have received and know the reality that Christ is our very life, we *want* to forgive those who have hurt us! We do *not* want to keep metabolizing the poison of an unforgiving attitude in our own souls.

The Truth Is Much Better!

A little review from an earlier chapter is helpful here. The Bible teaches that our own forgiveness by God is the basis for our forgiving others. Under the old covenant, people had to forgive in order to be forgiven. Jesus told them that if they didn't forgive others for the trespasses committed against them, then they wouldn't be forgiven (see Matthew 6:14-15). But everything changed upon the death of Jesus on the cross. The old covenant was in effect until He was crucified, but upon His crucifixion, the new covenant began (see Hebrews 9:17). *When Jesus Christ died, the new covenant began.* Remember, the new covenant doesn't start in Matthew 1:1. That's where New Testament Scriptures begin, but the new covenant itself started at the death of Jesus. That's what Hebrews 9 plainly teaches. We must properly interpret (or as one old translation says, "rightly divide") the Bible.

After Jesus died and the new covenant began, the Bible never again says that we must forgive to be forgiven. To the contrary, it says that we forgive because we *have* been forgiven. Colossians 3:13 says that *"just as the Lord forgave you,* so also should you." Paul wrote to the Ephesian church about this subject and said, "Be kind to one another, tenderhearted, forgiving each other, *just as God in Christ also has forgiven you"* (Ephesians 4:32).

What about this matter of forgiving *and forgetting?* Are we really required to forget the wrong things others have done to us? That's not what the Bible teaches. I suggested earlier that not even God does that. You may have raised your eyebrow in doubt about that statement, but it's true. The Bible doesn't say that He forgets our sins. It says that He doesn't *remember* them. Although many may think the two are the same thing, they aren't.

To forget means just that. It means we have no ability to bring to mind the forgotten thing. How could we possibly do that with some of the terrible hurts we've suffered in life? It's not possible. What we can do, though, is to *not remember*. As I've said, there's a big difference.

What does it mean to *remember?* Look at the word itself. It is comprised of two parts: *re-* and *member. Re-* is a prefix that means "to return to a previous condition" or "the repetition of a previous action." The word *member* means "one of a group; one that belongs, a part of the body." So the accurate and literal meaning of the word *remember* is to return something to a previous condition by making it belong to or join again with something. If I cut off my finger, the doctor may be able to *re-member* it if I get it to him in time.

The Bible doesn't say God forgets our sins. People sometimes talk about the *Sea of Forgetfulness,* but that phrase is not in the Bible. The idea was taken from Scripture, and it is found in Micah 7:19, where it says, "He will again have compassion on us; He will tread our iniquities under foot. Yes, You will cast all their sins into the depths of the sea." That's probably where the idea of a Sea of Forgetfulness comes from, but note that's not what the Bible says. It says He will separate our sins from us forever. He doesn't forget, but he does remember them no more. In other words, He will forever refuse to join our sins to us or our past guilt to Himself. He will not *re-member* them!

To illustrate the literal use of the word in a positive way, think about what Jesus said at the Last Supper to His disciples:

> The Lord Jesus in the night in which He was betrayed took bread; and when He had given thanks, He broke it and said, "This is My body, which is for you; do this in remembrance of Me." In the same way He took the cup also after supper, saying, "This cup is the new covenant in My blood; do this, as often as you drink it, in remembrance of Me" (1 Corinthians 11:23-25).

What did He mean by that? He meant, "As often as you partake of this communion meal in the future, do it in a way that you are appropriating the reality of your connection to Me." He wasn't telling believers that when we take communion, we are to think in our minds and pretend that we are there watching His crucifixion. He is telling us to *re-member*. We are to affirm by faith that we are inseparably joined to Him, and we affirm that reality again and again when we partake of the elements. Again, we are affirming—and yes, even experiencing—our union with Him on the cross in His burial and now in His resurrection life.

So our Father does not remember our sin anymore. Being omniscient means He knows everything, so He hasn't given up His omniscience and forgotten our sins. He simply refuses to ever "member them" to us or to Himself again.

That's what we are to do when it comes to forgiveness toward others. Do we forgive? Yes, but not because we must. We do it because we have been forgiven, and now we have the ability and the desire to forgive those who have hurt us.

Do we forget? No, but neither do we "remember." We release those who have hurt us from any obligations they have toward us, and we refuse to join the offense to us again. We may never forget, but as we walk in ongoing forgiveness, the event itself will have less and less emotional impact on us when we think about it. We will come to a place where, although we haven't forgotten, we don't feel the pain of the situation anymore because we have been healed.

Clarify Your Thinking

Don't set an impossible goal for yourself to forgive and forget. Your Father doesn't expect that of you. To forgive those who've hurt you will set you free from being bound to the event and will enable you to move toward healing. That's a good reason to do it.

It will allow you to get on with your life in a way that you're not contaminated in your attitude, mood, or perspective because of the past. That's a good reason to do it.

Most importantly, it will allow you to act in a way that is consistent with who you truly are—a loving, forgiving person whose desire is to honor your Father by giving to others the same forgiveness that you have received from Him. That's the *best* reason to do it.

Forgiveness is at the heart of the Christian faith and message. To joyfully and productively live out our faith is to extend to others the same forgiveness we've received. We may not forget, but we don't re-attach ourselves mentally to the event. We don't remember, and as a result, we walk in freedom—a kind of freedom that only those who have truly forgiven others may know.

Grace Is a
Very Important
Doctrine

I've intentionally left this final lie we've heard at church until last because it points to the heart of the whole book. The issue in each of
the lies we've considered together hinges on the topic of grace. All the
lies share legalistic undertones. Go back and look at all the lies discussed in this book, and you'll see that almost all of them suggest that
the focus is on you and what you should do or ought to be doing better. With legalism, it's all about *you,* but God's grace doesn't call attention to ourselves and our duties. It directs our focus to *Him* and what
He has already done!

Sadly, even the subject of grace itself is often misunderstood. There
are many errors made when it comes to teachings on this subject, but
in this final chapter, I want to address one of the most subtle lies about
grace. It suggests that grace is a very important doctrine. This may sound
like a compliment to grace, but it's not. It actually undermines it.

The great danger in this lie is that it sets the subject of grace on the
same level as other biblical doctrines. It's the idea that grace is just one
more topic in the Bible that we can study and benefit from learning.
That simply isn't true.

Sometimes I've spoken in churches where somebody will say to me,

"Our church is focusing on grace this whole year!" They mean that as a good thing, but I can't help but wonder, "What did you focus on last year? What will you focus on next year?"

Grace isn't another subject of the Bible. Grace is *the* subject of the Bible because grace is the essence of the gospel, and there's nothing as important in Scripture as the good news of what our triune God has accomplished through the finished work of the cross. The news of what happened at the cross *is* the gospel.

The apostle Paul defined his ministry as the responsibility and privilege to "testify solemnly of *the gospel of the grace of God*" (Acts 20:24). It was the good news of the grace of God that Paul declared. Grace wasn't simply another doctrine in his mind. It was the very DNA of the good news that God had entrusted him to share with his world.

The Truth Is So Much Better!

Paul felt so passionate about this gospel of grace that he said that nothing in his life had value greater than the privilege of sharing the exciting message of God's grace. If necessary, he was willing to die seeing to it that as many people as possible could know this good news.

That's the effect authentic grace still has in people's lives. Legalistic religion may cause a short-lived enthusiasm in people about one topic or another for a short time. Think about your own life. Have you found yourself excited about one thing and then another over the years? I remember when I first began to see the grace of God as I do today. I was thrilled but wondered, "Will this grow old like all the other things I've been excited about in the past?" That was in 1990, and I can tell you the answer to the question now from the vantage point of decades gone by. No, the grace of God is not a topic that you'll grow tired of after a long time.

There's a reason that we can stay energized by God's grace and not become accustomed to it the way we've become comfortable and maybe even casual about many things we've learned in our walk as believers. The reason can be found in what John said in describing

Jesus. He said about his own experience with Jesus, "We saw His glory, glory as of the only begotten from the Father, full of grace and truth" (John 1:14).

The reason we don't grow weary with grace when we really understand it is because we come to see that grace isn't simply a doctrine. Grace is personified in Jesus Christ, and we can never get over Him! He *is* grace.

If there's any doubt in your mind that grace is nothing less than the person of Christ Jesus, Himself, consider what Paul said to Titus about grace:

> For the *grace of God has appeared, bringing salvation to all men,* instructing us to deny ungodliness and worldly desires and to live sensibly, righteously, and godly in the present age, looking for the blessed hope and the appearing of the glory of our great God and Savior, Christ Jesus, who gave Himself for us to redeem us from every lawless deed, and to purify for Himself a people for His own possession, zealous for good deeds (Titus 2:11-14).

Paul said that *grace* appeared and brought salvation to all men. It's not a doctrine that did that, but a person. This person has saved us, and He now teaches us how to live, creating in us an eager desire for His return. Grace (Christ) causes us to be zealous about good deeds.

Sometimes I hear critics of the grace walk contend that grace teachers may cause people to move toward careless living. They're afraid grace might lead to licentiousness—a reckless lifestyle marked by poor behavior. Paul assures us that true grace won't do that.

However, I too have a concern. My concern is about those who profess to love the grace of God but approach it as if it is nothing more than another "important teaching" found in the Bible. Their approach to grace may be truly dangerous.

Why would I suggest that? It's because of the subtlety of their particular lie. If a person behaves sinfully, argues that they're under grace, and claims that's why it's okay for them to sin, we all know they've jumped the track.

On the other hand, if somebody embraces grace as a doctrine without realizing that it is the person of Jesus Christ, his error may go undetected. He can say all kinds of positive-sounding things about "the doctrine of grace," and nobody will think anything about it. Nobody, that is, except the enemy of our souls. He will stand on the sidelines of the church, giggling and clapping because Jesus Christ has become marginalized in His own church, and the church has reduced Him to nothing more than a doctrine.

Make no mistake about it: The enemy of our souls couldn't care less about your doctrine as long as he can cause you to shift your focus away from Jesus Christ. He will applaud your studious search for biblical doctrine if it will distract you from Christ Himself. He would just as soon see you caught up in religious behavior as he would sinful behavior. Perhaps he would prefer the former because the error of living a religious lifestyle that doesn't flow from an expression of Christ within us is much harder for us to recognize than it is for us to realize we're doing things that are blatantly and obviously sinful. Unrighteous behavior is glaring. Self-righteous behavior can look absolutely glamorous in our own eyes.

"So," our enemy would say, "take your doctrine of grace and run with it!" Just as long as we don't connect the dots between the topic we call *grace* and the person of Jesus, he is fine with that. He might even affirm that grace is a very important doctrine. "Study the subject if you want. Parse the Greek verbs. Read commentaries about it. Just don't make the connection that when we're talking about grace, we're talking about Jesus." That's how he thinks.

Clarify Your Thinking

To think clearly on this subject and on every other lie addressed in this book, it is important to come to the place where you see— where you *really* see—that every subject of the Bible, every focus in our lifestyles, everything we think, do, and say is to be grounded in Jesus Christ. It's not about behaving the right way. It's not about having a perfect understanding of the Bible. It's not about anything that we do or don't do. It's all about Him. He is grace, and He is the fountainhead of everything else in life.

Suggesting that grace is a very important doctrine is like saying that breathing is an important part of my life. That would be an understatement of ridiculous proportions. Breathing is not an "important" part of my life. Without it, there *is* no life!

Hebrews 12:15 says, "See to it that no one misses the grace of God" (NIV). That is so important. If we miss the grace of God by failing to understand that Christ *is* the grace of God given to humanity, we will be vulnerable to believing the lies discussed throughout this book. It is when we know the truth that we are set free to live. When you hear statements presented as biblical truth, ask the Holy Spirit to guide you into all truth and discernment. Evaluate what you hear by whether it is pointing your focus to Jesus Christ or to yourself. Does it direct your attention to what He has done or to what you're being told you should do?

Remember, grace is the unilateral lovingkindness of our Father, poured out on us through Jesus Christ. Look to Him, trust Him, and then live in the joyful freedom that can come only from Him.

If this book has encouraged you in your own grace walk, I'd like to invite you to visit my website at www.gracewalk.org, where you can find other resources I have developed. You may be particularly interested in the video series that covers 101 lies, not just the 52 you've read about in this book. (It turned out that 101 were too many for one book. But you can find out what all of them are on the website.)

I'd love to hear your thoughts about *52 Lies Heard in Church Every Sunday*. You may write me at...

Dr. Steve McVey
Grace Walk Ministries
PO Box 3669
Riverview, FL 33568

Other Books by Steve McVey

⌒∽

Grace Walk
Living the *grace walk* will get you off the religious roller coaster. Using his own journey from legalism into grace, Steve McVey illustrates the foundational, biblical truths of who you are in Jesus Christ and how you can let Him live His life through you each day.

As you experience your identity in Jesus Christ, you will come to know "Amazing Grace" as not just a song but as your true way of life.

Grace Rules
Understanding the concepts of law and grace can help you live out your identity in Christ. By discovering how Jesus' grace can consistently flow out of your life, you can experience a satisfying and abundant Christian life.

Walking in the Will of God
Rediscover the grace-filled, relational God of the Scriptures. Steve McVey demonstrates that a rule-focused life causes anxiety and distance from the Father. A relationship-based life brings security in His dependability. Knowing that God *wants* to guide you, you can relax and enjoy a bold, no-regrets life.

More Harvest House Books to Help You Grow

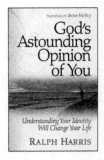

GOD'S ASTOUNDING OPINION OF YOU

Understanding Your Identity Will Change Your Life

Ralph Harris

Do you know that God's view of you is much greater than your own? Ralph Harris, founder and President of Life-Course Ministries, leads you to embrace the Scriptures' truth about what God thinks of you—that you are holy, righteous, blameless, and lovable.

With clear and simple explanations and examples, this resource will help you turn toward the love affair with God you were created for...a relationship in which you

- exchange fear and obligation for delight and devotion
- recognize the remarkable role and strength of the Holy Spirit in your daily life
- view your status as a *new creation* as the "new normal"— and live accordingly!

Knowing the Heart of the Father

Four Experiences with God That Will Change Your Life

David Eckman

You're stuffed full of Christian information. But where is God in all of it?

Perhaps Christianity seems irrelevant to where your heart is really at. Maybe you're thirsting for a *felt experience* of the Bible's truth. What if you could...

1. have an all-encompassing sense that you have a loving heavenly Dad?
2. have a sense of being enjoyed and delighted in by Him?
3. recognize that He sees you differently than you see yourself?
4. realize that *who you are* is more important to Him than *what you do?*

Do you want things to be different? See how these four great heart/soul transformations result in a vibrant, living faith that can stand up to the tests of life.